# Captain of the Discovery

# Captain of the Discovery

## The Story of Captain George Vancouver

Roderick Haig-Brown
*Illustrated by Gordon MacLean*

Macmillan of Canada/Toronto

ISBN  0-7705-1060-4 *Cloth*

0-7705-1061-2 *Paper*

First published in 1956 as Volume 9 in the *Great Stories
of Canada* series by Macmillan of Canada; reprinted
1959, 1964, 1967; revised 1974

Printed in Canada

# Contents

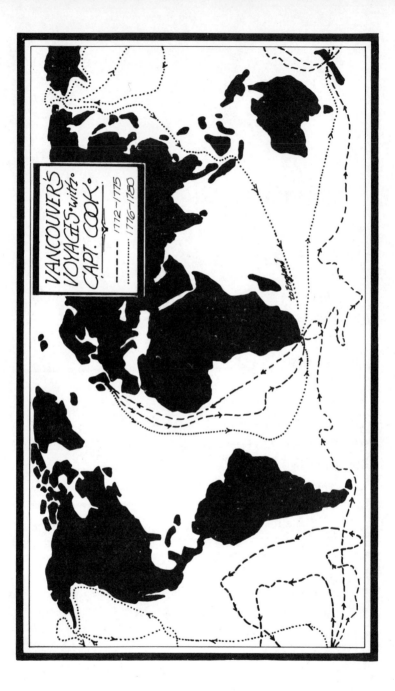

VANCOUVER'S
VOYAGES·with·
CAPT. COOK·

— 1772–1775
···· 1776–1780

to England

# 1. Boy Seaman

GEORGE VANCOUVER first went to sea when he was just fifteen. He signed as able seaman aboard the naval sloop *Resolution*, fitting in the London dockyards for a voyage of exploration. But he stowed his gear in the gun-room and took his orders and discipline from the gunner, because he was really an officer cadet, sent aboard with a "letter of service" from the Admiralty requesting the captain to show him "such kindness as you shall judge fit for a gentleman, both in accommodating him in your ship and in furthering his improvement." This meant that in addition to learning seamanship in the usual way, he would study mathematics and navigation under the ship's schoolmaster and possibly under the captain himself. In time, if he behaved himself and learned his duty, he would become a midshipman; still later he would be allowed to write the examinations for promotion to commissioned rank.

No ship in the world could have offered young Vancouver better naval instruction than the *Resolution*. Her "schoolmaster" was her astronomer, William Wales, a brilliant mathematician who later, as master of mathematics at Christ's Hospital School, London, trained a whole generation of naval officers. He was strict and exacting, very quick with a stick or the rope's end, but quicker still with jokes and enthusiasm and excitement; it would have been a dull boy who could not learn from him.

The ship's captain, and leader of the expedition, which she made up with her consort the *Adventure*, was Captain James Cook R.N., the greatest seaman and navigator of his day, perhaps of all time. Cook, the son of a Yorkshire farm labourer, was already famous for his surveys of the St. Lawrence River under the French guns, for his special appointment as King's Surveyor to chart the coasts of Newfoundland and Labrador, and for his first great voyage around the world. Many of the men who had sailed with him on this first voyage were with him again now, and George Vancouver heard their tales of the warm and lovely South Sea Islands, of the fierce dangers of the Great Barrier Reef and of hazardous exploration and discovery along the coasts of New Zealand and Australia.

On the 13th July, 1772, the expedition sailed from Plymouth Sound for the Cape of Good Hope, at the southern tip of Africa. The voyage to the Cape by way of the island of Madeira and across the equator took over ten weeks, and Vancouver began to learn something of the ways of the navy, and of Captain Cook's ways in particular. In his home at the Norfolk seaport of King's Lynn, where his father was the customs officer, he had often been aboard the trading vessels that came in from faraway places. They had seemed to him then fine tall ships, manned by stout

2

seamen under firm discipline. But there were important differences in the navy ships. *Resolution* and *Adventure* stood three eight-hour watches each day instead of the usual twelve-hour watch and watch, and he learned that this was to guard the health of the men by giving them more frequent chances to put on dry clothes and warm up. Every phase of living—eating, sleeping and the working of the ship—was governed by strict orders, rigidly obeyed. This also, he quickly learned, was for the safety of the ship and the health of the crew. For there were two enemies to be fought in any long voyage: the sea and disease.

Of the two the more dangerous by far was disease, and one disease in particular—scurvy. The sea might claim a man, as it had claimed the carpenter's mate of the *Resolution* when he fell overboard in the North Atlantic; it might destroy a ship and her whole crew, as the Great Barrier Reef had almost destroyed Cook's *Endeavour* on his previous voyage. But these were chances that skill and watchfulness could prevent. Scurvy crept in with relentless persistence among the crew of every ship that undertook a long voyage. Men became pale and tired and careless in their work; their hair fell out, their teeth twisted and dropped from bleeding gums; their bones thickened and knotted, and very often they died. Scurvy was the deep-sea sailor's fate, and until Cook's time few had escaped it. Yet Cook had brought the *Endeavour*'s crew home from a three-year voyage with every man in good health.

We know now that scurvy is caused by lack of Vitamin C, the vitamin found mainly in fresh fruits and vegetables. Cook did not know this, but he was sure that food played an important part; he believed that dirt and dampness had something to do with it and that stale water,

3

skimmings of salt beef, too much oatmeal and too much oil made it worse, if they did not cause it. So Vancouver found himself taking weekly salt-water baths with the other seamen, washing his clothes whenever the weather was good enough, airing bedding, scrubbing down decks with vinegar as disinfectant, tending fires to dry out quarters or burning gunpowder to fumigate the ship. And at mealtimes strange new foods were on the tables with the salt beef and biscuits—sauerkraut and potable broth and marmalade of carrots. Many of the seamen did not care for them, but they ate them on pain of prompt punishment. Long before they reached the Cape, Vancouver had seen two men stripped to the waist and flogged for refusing to eat proper rations.

These were important lessons that he could have learned on no other ship. "Seamen will refuse a new diet," Cook said, "simply because it is new, no matter how much good it may do them; the only way they can be persuaded to accept it is by the authority and example of the commander." He did not hesitate to use both authority and example in this and all other matters.

The ships reached the Cape of Good Hope with the crews in good health, took on water and supplies there and sailed again late in November on the real purpose of the voyage—the search through the lonely, stormy, ice-bound reaches of the southern ocean for a continent that was supposed to be there.

November in the southern hemisphere is late spring, but Cook was searching southward, towards the Antarctic Circle, and they were soon in cold and bad weather. Extra clothing and extra rum rations were issued to the crews, but the firm discipline was maintained. Soon they were among icebergs, with clear ice thickly coated on rigging and bulwarks. George Vancouver learned the bitter hardship of going aloft under such conditions, of wrestling frozen canvas with frozen, bleeding hands, chipping ice free from blocks and from ropes that would not run through them, of coming off watch into quarters that were damp and mouldering in spite of all that could be done to keep them aired and dry. But "the people", as Cook called his crew, worked cheerfully and well under the harsh conditions, completely confident of the skill and purpose of their leader.

Cook's purpose was perfectly clear in his own mind and he drove his ships boldly to search out and prove or disprove every previous rumour of a southern continent, then drove again where no ships had ever been to test a theory of his own that there might be a mass of land near the pole. On January 17th, 1773, the two ships crossed the invisible line of the Antarctic Circle, making Cook and his people the first men in history to do so. It was a clear day and in the enthusiasm of their achievement they pressed on farther south. By mid-afternoon thirty-eight huge icebergs were in sight. By six-thirty p.m. the ice-pack was solid ahead of them and they turned back from latitude 67° 15′, to trace out another line of search northward and eastward towards land recently sighted by another expedition.

So the search continued, back to the ice again and steadily eastward through February and March. They met with fog and bad weather and always ice and more ice. Nowhere in all this waste of ocean was there a chance to find fresh supplies, but Cook soon found that the icebergs were fresh water, with only a thin coating of salt on the outside, so he kept his ships in good water. Danger was constant. Fogs crept in upon them so suddenly and swiftly that they were often sailing blindly among the icebergs. Once, when William Wales and Mr. Foster, the botanist of the expedition, went out in a small boat to take temperature readings, a thick fog came down and they were lost for several hours. They stayed where they were and one of the ships found them in the end, but it was a grim warning of what could happen in that desolation of barren cold.

Early in February a violent storm separated the two ships. For three days Cook beat up and down, firing a gun every half-hour and burning flares at night. But the signals were not answered and the only thing to do was go on and hope that the *Adventure* would sail ahead safely to the agreed meeting-place at Queen Charlotte Sound in New Zealand. The lonely search was now doubly dangerous, since there could be no hope of rescue if the *Resolution* should be wrecked in the ice.

By the middle of March the weather was too bad to continue much longer so far south. The *Resolution*'s people were nearly all suffering from chilblains, signs of scurvy were beginning to appear and altogether they were an exhausted crew. Cook decided it was time to sail for New Zealand, where he could hope to find fresh food and rest for the men. Towards the end of the month the ship anchored in Dusky Bay, after 117 days at sea and ten thousand miles of search. As soon as the ship was riding safely, every sailor put his hook and line overboard and began to haul in fish. The first stage of the hard and dangerous search was over.

George Vancouver was already on the way to becoming a toughened seaman. He had seen storm and fog and danger, had suffered hardship and tested his health and strength against the demands of the sea. More important still, he had seen Cook tried by the problems of his search, balancing the health and strength of his men, the safety and condition of his ships exactly against the needs of his mission, so that everything was used to the limits of risk and endurance and nothing that could be done was left undone. And at every stage William Wales had explained the difficulties, drawn the lessons and made the young gentlemen of the gun-room work out the problems of navigation. They learned to take their own sights of the sun and stars and their own readings of the ships' chronometers, the new and superbly accurate timepieces which were being fully tested for the first time.

Now, with ships and men strained to the limit, it was time to learn how health and condition could be restored from the resources of those wild, unexplored and unsettled regions.

# 2. South Seas

THE *Resolution* stayed on in Dusky Bay, on the southeast corner of the South Island of New Zealand, all through April. Cook's first care was to clear up all traces of the scurvy that threatened. He had hoped to find scurvy grass and wild celery and other vegetables, but there were none, so he had beer brewed from the leaves of spruce trees. This, with an abundance of fresh fish and wild-fowl, soon restored the health and spirits of the men.

There was work to be done. The water casks were filled and wood was cut for fuel. The forge was sent ashore for the blacksmiths to work on repairs, and more trees were felled, so that the carpenters could make new spars and repair sea damage to bulwarks and decks and hatch covers. But time was made for the men to go ashore, for parties to go out to hunt ducks and geese, and for the several arms of the bay to be explored. For the first time, young Vancouver set foot on newly discovered land, where no white man had been

8

before him. He trod among great trees, covered with vines and creepers, utterly unlike any he had known in England; he saw waterfalls and snow-capped mountains and forest that stretched away beyond farthest sight.

They had supposed at first that the bay was uninhabited but a few of the native Maoris were seen in the first week or so. Cook made every possible effort to win their friendship, leaving medals and beads and mirrors and even hatchets, which were considered great treasures by most native peoples, where they would be sure to find them. But they remained shy and kept their distance until a hunting-party fell in with a man and two women one day. Cook spoke to them in scraps of native language he had learned at Tahiti on his previous voyage, and they waited for the party and became friendly, even though they could not understand. He gave them presents and rubbed noses with the man, and there was more conversation which neither side could understand while Hodges, the artist of the expedition, sketched the natives. A few days later Cook gave the man a cloak of red baize which he had had made up aboard the ship. The man received the gift in full Maori ceremonial dress and showed his friendship and appreciation by giving Cook his patta pattou, the war-club he carried at his waist. Cook took these pains in winning the confidence of even one man in the hope of making it easier and safer for ships that came to the bay in the future.

At the end of April they sailed for Queen Charlotte Sound and on May 18 found the *Adventure* safely at anchor there. It was a happy and cheerful reunion after fourteen weeks of separation in those lonely and dangerous places, but the crew of the *Adventure* was in bad shape. Her commander, Captain Furneaux, had little of Cook's driving energy and even less of his faith in the precautions against scurvy, so many of his men were suffering from the disease. Cook took charge immediately. He went ashore himself and soon found plenty of wild celery and scurvy grass. In no time at all great quantities of both were harvested and taken aboard the ships. Within three weeks the crews of both ships were in condition to go to sea again, and though it was still winter Cook decided to continue his search through the unknown seas to the east, between New Zealand and South America.

A month later the *Adventure* had scurvy again. On a calm day late in July Cook crossed to her and found her cook dead and twenty of her best men sick. Aboard the *Resolution* only one man had signs of scurvy. Patiently, Cook explained again the routines of diet and sent one of his own seamen aboard to do the cooking. Then, since he felt satisfied there could be no great mass of land between New Zealand and South America, he decided to sail for Tahiti, the loveliest of the South Sea Islands, to lay in a good store of fresh supplies and give the crews a longer rest.

The next two or three months were a young boy's dream of all that adventure at sea should be, as the ships stopped at one after another of the lovely tropical islands. Perhaps Tahiti was best of all, where Cook was welcomed as a returning hero and carried shoulder-high ashore. There was warm sunshine after the Antarctic cold, and good fresh food of all kinds in abundance—coconuts, plantains, bananas, yams and other fresh vegetables, which soon restored the health of the crews, and plenty of fine fat hogs for fresh meat. The native people were handsome and friendly, the men brown and muscular, the women and girls full of laughter and gaiety. There was singing and dancing and native entertainment, and Vancouver watched Cook's careful and courteous negotiations with the important chiefs. Every formality was observed and all members of the ships' crews were warned to do nothing that would offend native customs or provoke quarrels. Vancouver met the young king, Otoo, for the first time and began a friendship with him—the first of many friendships with native kings and chiefs that were to help him when he commanded his own ship on exploration and discovery.

But though Cook was considerate and fair in all his dealings with the native peoples, he insisted that they should return courtesy for courtesy and good behaviour for fair dealing. Nearly all the natives they dealt with were natural—and highly skilful—thieves until checked. In the first few days at Tahiti the ships were invaded by undisciplined mobs, under men who claimed to be chiefs but who abused the captain's hospitality by themselves stealing. Cook was so angry with one of these that he fired two shots over his head as he was nearing shore in his canoe. The man immediately jumped overboard and a boat was sent to take the canoe; but the natives on shore began to throw rocks, so Cook ordered one of the ship's big guns fired, which chased them off, then followed himself in a second boat and picked up two canoes. A few hours later the canoes were given back and all was forgiven; but the stealing was kept within bounds from then on.

From Tahiti they went to the Society Islands, where Cook was welcomed by his old friend Oree, the chief. Soon after their arrival one of the botanists was attacked while on shore and stripped of all clothes. Oree at once offered himself as a hostage and insisted on staying aboard the *Resolution* until the clothes were recovered. From the same island Captain Furneaux took a native named Omai aboard and eventually brought him to London, where he met Samuel Johnson and many other great people of that day before being returned safely to his own island.

It is impossible to describe all the adventures and happenings of that South Sea winter, or all the islands the ships visited. Towards the beginning of October, which was the start of the southern spring, they turned southward for New Zealand. They were soon in bad weather and once again the ships were separated, this time for good. Cook waited many days at the meeting-place in Queen Charlotte Sound, but eventually sailed alone. The *Adventure* came in a few days later and found the messages he had left. But when they were almost ready to leave, one of the boats, which had been sent out to gather wild celery, failed to come back.

The following morning Captain Furneaux sent out another boat, with a full crew and ten marines. After searching far up the inlet they came to a sandy beach where several large canoes were drawn up. Two men ran away from the canoes, so they landed and quickly found grim evidence of what had happened. In one canoe were oarlocks from the boat and a pair of shoes belonging to one of the midshipmen. Nearby were a number of baskets containing roasted human flesh. What had happened was all too clear. But they knew they had to go on to make sure that none of the boat's crew was still living.

Round the next point they came upon a Maori village, with many canoes moored in front of it and almost two thousand people gathered on the beach. Mr. Burney, the second lieutenant of the *Adventure*, who was in charge of the boat, ordered the marines to fire a succession of volleys until all the natives had run off into the woods. Then they landed again and at once found the bodies of their murdered shipmates, battered and mutilated, sprawled near the last bundles of celery they had cut and carried down to the beach. Burney's men were too few for him to press his attack farther, but he destroyed as many of the canoes as possible and fired another volley when the natives threatened to attack to save their canoes. By this time it was raining heavily, half the ammunition was spent and much of the powder that remained was damp. Reluctantly, Burney decided there was nothing to do but return to the ship with his terrible news. Short-handed now and discouraged, Furneaux decided to sail for England, which he reached in July of 1774.

Cook and the people of the *Resolution*, knowing nothing of all this, continued southward, cheerfully accepting the risk of exploring alone through the ice and cold of the Antarctic Circle. They were a confident crew, proud of themselves and their captain, in perfect health and willing to face any hardship or danger. Soon the rigging was coated with ice again, the sails were frozen stiff and as hard to handle as sheets of metal; icebergs, some of them two hundred feet high and two or three miles in width, were on every side. Cook ran steadily southward among them, using every art of seamanship, until a solid wall of ice turned him. From there he made a long track northward to the latitude of New Zealand, then southward again to 71°, the farthest southward penetration of the voyage and the farthest, Cook believed, that any man would ever want to go.

At the moment Cook ordered the ship put about towards the north again, young George Vancouver was standing well forward, looking over the broken chaos of the ice-pack. No man in the world's history had been so far south before. No man before had seen what he was seeing now. He glanced aft towards the quarter-deck, then ducked forward and ran swiftly up the easy slope of the bowsprit. Right at the end he turned and waved his cap, a tiny figure swinging with the ship's movement against the fearful background of ice. History says he yelled out a Latin tag: "Ne plus ultra." Perhaps he did; boys in those days knew their Latin pretty well. But what he meant was: "This is it! As far as we go! And I've been farther south than any of you."

The dangers of navigation through the ice with a flimsy wooden sailing ship were constant, but the captain and crew met them with such skill and confidence that they became routine. Even with a hundred or two hundred icebergs in sight, Cook would carry sail through the daylight hours, then calmly set his ship to drift among them through the brief darkness. But there was one incident Vancouver never forgot.

It was in the dinner-hour and all the officers and men except the watch were below at their meal. The ship was sailing briskly, carrying a fair quantity of sail on a moderate breeze. There was a sudden call for all hands on deck. Officers and men rushed up from every part of the ship, then stood frozen with horror. The officer of the watch had attempted to pass down-wind, instead of safely up-wind, of an enormous iceberg. He had misjudged the drift of the iceberg and now the ship was rushing straight into the line of its drift. It was too late to change course or bring the

ship about. After the frozen moment in which he had assessed the situation, Cook gave a few sharp orders which sent men into the rigging to trim the sails to best advantage and others to pick up spars and stand by to fend off the iceberg. But every man, including Cook, knew that he was staring death in the face. The ship rushed on, meeting the drift of the iceberg. Cliffs and pinnacles of gleaming blue ice towered two hundred feet above them. The cold breath of the iceberg touched them and they waited for the shock of the strike that would topple the masts and tear the bottom out of the ship. None came. Miraculously the ship swept past within inches of the underwater danger, to dance crazily in the back surge of sea behind the ice mass.

This, then, was George Vancouver's early training in the skills and dangers of the sea. It continued through another winter among the tropical islands and still another summer of exploration, past Cape Horn and round to meet the first southward track they had made from the Cape of Good Hope three years before. England was sighted again on 29th July, 1775, and the ship anchored off the Isle of Wight. George Vancouver was eighteen now and a midshipman; he was also what he had not been when he signed on—a seaman.

# 3. Death of a Leader

ON HIS return to England Cook's great achievements were recognized by the Admiralty, which made him Captain of Greenwich Seamen's Hospital, a post that paid an excellent salary for shore duty. The Royal Society elected him a fellow and awarded him its Gold Medal for his success in the prevention of scurvy. Cook was happily married, with three sons, and it seemed that all he had to do now was to settle down to an easier yet still useful life ashore.

But the *Resolution* was already being refitted for another voyage of exploration and Cook was constantly called upon for advice. It soon appeared that the ship was to be sent to the Pacific again, this time to search for a northwest passage, the seaway through the north American continent from Atlantic to Pacific that was still believed to exist. Early in 1776, because there was no other man nearly so well fitted for the job, Cook was asked to command the expedition. He accepted immediately and was appointed next day; that evening he went aboard the *Resolution* and hoisted his captain's pennant. His old crews flocked to join him. Among them was Midshipman George Vancouver, returned from visiting his family at King's Lynn.

On July 12th, 1776, with a new consort, the little *Discovery* of two hundred and thirty tons, the *Resolution* sailed from Plymouth harbour. George Vancouver was aboard the *Discovery*, under the command of Lieutenant Clerke, who had served with Cook on the two previous voyages. They made an uneventful but rather slow passage by the Cape of Good Hope to New Zealand, anchoring in Queen Charlotte Sound on Feb. 12th, 1777.

Cook stayed only briefly in New Zealand, but he took time to investigate as well as he could the deaths of the *Adventure*'s boat crew. George Vancouver had already seen him many times deal with strange native peoples and his bravery, coolness and patience gave him extraordinary power with them. Often he would land alone to meet them, unarmed. If they threatened him he would quietly sit down and throw them beads, knives or other small presents, occasionally moving nearer, never showing the least uncertainty or impatience. In the end they would forget their fear, lay down their own arms and talk with him as best they could, by signs or in South Sea words that were common to most of the islands.

He went ashore now with Omai as interpreter, among a people afraid and expecting punishment. He questioned calmly and patiently until he learned, as he had expected all along, that the attack was not planned but had happened in a sudden flare of anger and fear over some petty quarrel. Once he was satisfied this was so, he forgave them without punishment.

Leaving New Zealand, they were still hopeful of reaching the northwest coast of America in time for a summer of exploration. But adverse winds held them back and they became very short of fodder and water for the livestock that they were carrying to establish domestic animals in Tahiti. The first islands they reached had little to offer and they had to swing over to the Friendly Islands to save the lives of the animals. Cook was now six months behind in his sailing plan and realized he could not hope to do any work on the northern coast-line that year. He called at Tahiti to renew his friendship with Otoo and to deliver the cows, horses and sheep that had been sent out to him, then decided to continue his exploration of the mid-Pacific.

The first discovery was made on Christmas Eve—a low-lying sandy atoll which was named Christmas Island. It was important only because they found turtles there in great numbers. Cook sent several boats ashore and the men caught over three hundred, a very valuable supply because they could be kept alive on board ship with very little attention until needed.

Three weeks later, in January of 1778, they discovered the Hawaiian Islands, which Cook named the Sandwich Islands. It was an important discovery. Here, in an apparently empty ocean, was fertile and fruitful land, where ships could put in to find water and supplies. And it was important to the present expedition, as a wintering and supply base a full month's sailing nearer the coast they were to explore.

As soon as the ships were anchored off the island of Kauai, natives came aboard in great numbers. They understood the Tahitian language, but they had no knowledge of iron or beads or other trading goods, and it was quite evident they had never seen sailing ships or white men before. They examined everything aboard the ships with great curiosity, openly taking what they wanted until they were told it was wrong. After that they behaved very well until one young fellow stole the knife out of the galley, jumped overboard and swam through the surf. The boats put off to stop him and even fired two or three shots, but he got safely ashore.

Lieutenant Williamson, who was in charge of the boats, followed ashore to look for water. As they touched, many natives came down to them and one tried to seize Williamson's gun. Williamson shot him dead, then ordered the boats to the ship.

Cook was furious when he heard of it and at once landed in another boat at the same place. He ordered everyone to stay in the boat, handed his gun to one of the men and stepped ashore with only his cutlass at his side. The natives at once fell flat on their faces in worship, and it was later learned that they believed Cook to be their god Lono, come to visit them.

After that everything went smoothly and the ships successfully watered and provisioned at Waimea as well as Kauai. They left the islands in February, sailing north and east to reach the coast of America off northern California early in March.

It was Cook's intention to follow the coast-line northward so closely that he would be sure to find and explore any opening that could possibly be a northwest passage. At least three such possibilities were commonly shown on the charts of the day—the Straits of Juan de Fuca, the Strait of de Fonte and the Strait of Anian. A reward of £20,000 was waiting in England for the first captain and crew to discover the passage and every man aboard both ships had a clear idea of the importance of the mission.

But the coast-line, its weather, its dangers and its possible harbours were all virtually unknown. Sir Francis Drake had followed it as far as northern Washington in 1579, naming the land New Albion and claiming it for Queen Elizabeth. The Spaniards had made one or two daring voyages northward from Mexico; in 1774 Juan Perez had reached the Queen Charlotte Islands, and a year later Don Bruno Hecata in the *Santiago* and Lieutenant Quadra in the 27-foot schooner *Sonora* had made a landing near Gray's Harbour in the State of Washington. Quadra, in his tiny ship, had sailed on to 57°N. and made another landing on Dall Island, north of the Queen Charlottes. Admiral Bering of Russia had reached Alaska and sighted Mt. St. Elias on his second voyage in 1741. But none of these adventures had yielded much information, and Cook planned his first season's work as a broad survey rather than a determined effort to find the passage.

They were able to follow the coasts of Oregon and Washington in fairly good weather, but off northern Washington a succession of bad storms forced them out to sea and they passed without finding the entrance to the Strait of Juan de Fuca, though Cook saw and named Cape Flattery, the southern point of the entrance.

As the weather eased they stood towards the coast again and George Vancouver saw for the first time the timbered hills and mountains of the great island that was to bear his name. No one knew it as an island at that time, but as soon as the ships were near the coast Indians with broad, flat faces and high cheek-bones came off to meet them in carved and painted canoes. Since they needed new masts and rigging, as well as fresh water and any fresh supplies that might be available, Cook put into Nootka Sound and found safe anchorage in Friendly Cove. The Indians behaved well under the orders of the chief, Maquinna, and traded willingly, offering the skins of many animals, especially sea-otters, and human skulls which they claimed were those of enemies they had eaten. In spite of this grim evidence of their prowess, Cook explored the Sound and went freely ashore among them with his usual calm interest, learning as much as he could of their nature and their way of life.

But they had delayed there for necessary work rather than for exploration and Cook sailed away as soon as the ships were ready, straight into another violent storm. The storm drove them far off the land and when good sailing weather came Cook felt there was no time to close in again and search for the Strait of de Fonte. They sailed steadily northwestward and soon were off the coast of Alaska, discovering Prince William Sound and Cook's River. From there they worked on round the Alaska peninsula, then northward again, often through heavy fog, across Bristol Bay and into Bering Strait. Early in August they crossed the Arctic Circle. By the end of the month they were north of 70°, with a solid ice wall ahead and drift ice threatening to close them in. They turned southward, to winter and refit in the Hawaiian Islands, sighting them again late in November after a long and difficult voyage.

This time they came upon two new islands, Maui and the main island of Hawaii. After sailing round the big island to examine its coast-line, the ships finally put in at Karakakoa Bay, where there was a large settlement of natives and excellent anchorage.

22

Cook was welcomed with the same deep reverence shown to him on the other islands and soon became very friendly with the king, Terreeoboo, a wise, calm and dignified old man who supplied their needs very generously. But after about three weeks the attitude of the natives began to change. Even the king began to ask when the ships would be leaving. The natives would stroke the sailors and pat their bellies, suggesting by signs that they were in good shape again and it was time to go. The truth was that the demands of the ships were rapidly exhausting the local supplies and the islanders were afraid they would be short of their own needs.

Cook understood this point and sympathized with them. He put to sea on February sixth to find some other safe anchorage where he could continue to refit and take provisions. But the ships ran straight into a fierce gale and the *Resolution* had two sails split and her foremast badly damaged. Because he knew of no other safe place nearby, Cook put back into Karakakoa Bay.

There was no welcome this time. Instead of a thousand canoes, each and every one of them loaded with natives, putting out to meet the ships, the landing parties found only a few people on the beaches and these offered no welcome. The priests, they said, had tabooed the bay. The king and most of the people had left. But Terreeoboo knew the ships had put back in and was already returning.

He arrived the next day and Cook tried, not too successfully, to explain what had happened. But the king watched the mast being taken out of the ship and towed ashore for repairs and accepted the situation with a dignified courtesy, though not with enthusiasm.

By now the natives had returned to the bay in large numbers and were all about the ships. There had been trouble before with stealing, but it had been minor pilfering for the most part and fairly easily checked. Now it was a constant nuisance and rapidly passed beyond control. On the afternoon of February 13th, three days after the ships had anchored, a native was caught stealing the armourer's tongs from the *Discovery*. Cook ordered him flogged. But an hour or two later another native stole the tongs and escaped overboard to a canoe.

A boat was sent in immediate pursuit under Edgar, the master of the *Discovery*, with Midshipman Vancouver second in command. The canoe reached shore well ahead of them and the natives jumped out and ran off towards the hills. Edgar ran his boat into the beach and seized the canoe. Unluckily it belonged to an important chief, Pareea, who came up to claim it; and there was a fight, in which Pareea was knocked down by a hard blow on the head from an oar. As soon as this happened other natives, standing nearby, joined in. They threw rocks, then closed in with clubs and knives, forcing the crew away so that they could strip all the equipment from the boat. Vancouver, shielding Edgar, was knocked down in the water and lost his cap. But Pareea came to and ordered the natives back. He recovered some of the equipment, returned it to Edgar and Vancouver and told them to pull away from the shore and back to the ship. Then he followed in his own canoe, apologizing for what had happened and asking if Cook would kill him or allow him to come safely aboard the ships next day. Edgar told him he would be welcomed in friendship and the two rubbed noses.

In spite of the peaceful outcome, Cook was worried by what had happened. He felt Edgar had acted wrongly in seizing the canoe and that the natives would think the outcome a victory and become over-confident. He ordered all the islanders out of the ships and had a double guard posted by Lieutenant King's party, which was repairing the mast and sails on shore.

During the night one of the *Discovery*'s boats was stolen from her moorings. Cook took action immediately. He ordered all the remaining boats to be fully armed and manned, and stationed them across the bay to stop all movement. Two large canoes, which were trying to escape before the boats were posted, were stopped by a few shots from the big guns. King was ordered to keep the natives quiet on his side of the bay by promising that no one would be hurt, and to keep his people together and ready. Cook himself loaded his double-barrelled gun and started out for shore in the pinnace, with Lieutenant Phillips and nine marines. He was going to find King Terreeoboo and persuade him to come aboard as a hostage until the *Discovery*'s boat was returned. Lieutenant Williamson in the *Resolution*'s launch, also well-armed, was ordered to stand by the landing-place.

When Cook landed the natives bowed down respectfully before him as usual; but he was in a hot-tempered mood and determined to show that he meant business, so he ordered the marines to disembark and draw up on the shore. Then, with Lieutenant Phillips, he marched up to the village and asked for Terreeoboo and his two sons. When Terreeoboo came Cook told him he knew he had nothing to do with the disappearance of the *Discovery*'s boat, but asked if he and his sons would come aboard as his guests until it was recovered. Terreeoboo agreed at once and they started down the hill through the crowd of two or three thousand natives who had gathered.

It was a surly crowd, murmuring and moving restlessly, but it was not the first time Cook had faced such a situation and he was fearless and confident as always, moving slowly so that Terreeoboo would not be hurried, treating the old king as a brother chieftain and in no way as a prisoner. The men in the crowd surrounding them were mostly armed with pahooas, short stabbing knives, but there was nothing unusual in this and Cook was certain that a few shots from his marines would promptly check any threatening attack.

They were almost down to the waterside before anything went wrong. Then an old woman, one of the king's wives, came up and begged Terreeoboo with tears not to go on board the ship. At the same moment two chiefs took hold of him and made him sit down on the ground. Boats were moving out in the bay and the big guns of the ships began firing. The enormous crowd pressed in around the white men and their king, and the nine marines were surrounded by two or three thousand natives. Still calmly, Cook ordered Phillips to get the marines out of the crowd and line them on the rocks at the water's edge. The natives moved back willingly and made way for them to go through, but Cook looked down at Terreeoboo and saw that the old man was frightened and confused. Some of the natives were collecting their spears and putting on their protective war-mats. Cook turned to Phillips and told him they would have to leave the king, because it would be impossible to move him farther without firing and killing a number of the natives.

Cook's next intention was to call in the boats and get the marines back aboard them. But as he moved to do this a

native warrior came up behind him, threatening him with his pahooa and a stone held in his other hand. Cook immediately fired a load of bird-shot from the right barrel of his gun, but the charge was stopped by the man's protective mat. At the same moment another warrior rushed Phillips, who knocked him down with the butt of his gun. The crowd began to throw stones and a marine was knocked down. Cook moved back into the crowd. Another threatened him and Cook shot him dead with the load of ball from his left barrel. He ordered the marines to fire a volley and called out: "Take to the boats."

Before the marines could reload, the crowd rushed them. Four went down at once, but Midshipman Roberts moved the pinnace in smartly and opened fire in support. With the crowd pressing on him, Cook turned and walked slowly towards the water, signalling the boats to cease firing and move in close. Roberts held the pinnace in so that Phillips and the surviving marines reached it. But Williamson in the launch misunderstood the order and moved out.

Alone on shore, Cook was now at the water's edge. A native clubbed him from behind, and knocked him down. As he struggled to get up another stabbed him in the neck with his pahooa, so that he fell forward, face down in the water. As soon as he fell there was a great shout from the crowd. A steady hail of stones forced the boats to keep away, even though the great guns of the *Resolution* were fired. The natives who could reach Cook dragged him out of the water onto the rocks, where they stabbed him repeatedly and beat him to death with stones.

# 4. Lieut. George Vancouver, R.N.

CAPTAIN COOK'S loss was a deadening shock to all his officers and men. Many had been with him since the start of his first great voyage. Many, like Vancouver, had known no other commander. They trusted him and depended on him and were prepared to follow him wherever he chose to lead, not only because he was the supremely successful seaman, honoured and recognized by seamen everywhere, but because they had seen with their own eyes, time and again, just what he could do. They had seen him run under full sail, through foggy nights along an unknown coast, and sleep quietly through it all; they had seen him come suddenly on deck, when no one suspected danger, and change the course of the ship to safety; things like these had happened so often that his people believed he could sense and avoid danger instinctively. And they knew him as utterly fearless, a man who became only more serene, steadier and more cheerful as danger mounted, raising the spirits of everyone about him to meet it.

Now they were suddenly deprived of him and they could not believe it. Even Captain Clerke, who succeeded to the command, felt doubt of himself. He was very sick with tuberculosis and felt this was an additional handicap. But the ships and crews were still in danger. He transferred his command from *Discovery* to *Resolution* and set about strengthening their position.

The first essential was to bring the *Resolution*'s mast and sails off from shore, because without them the ship would be almost useless. William Bligh, master of the *Resolution* and a tough, brave man, was sent to help Lieutenant King with this. He found King's little encampment surrounded, with more natives, armed and threatening, steadily arriving from the village. As soon as Bligh and his men were ashore in a good defensive position the natives attacked with stones. The marines fired and killed or wounded several of them, forcing the rest to retreat behind rock-piles they had built. King then arranged a truce and got the mast and sails safely back to the ships.

King, whom the natives believed to be Cook's son, went ashore again that afternoon, to try to arrange for the surrender of Cook's body. Midshipman Vancouver followed him, in charge of the supporting boat. The natives expected them to attack and met them with a shower of stones, but as soon as King raised a white flag they broke into cries of joy and laid aside their spears and mats. An old priest, Koah, swam off to King's boat, also carrying a white flag. King told him he had come to demand Cook's body or else declare war. Koah promised the body would be brought at once and swam back to shore, shouting to the other natives that they were friends again. After a long wait King became impatient and sent Vancouver back to tell Clerke what had happened and ask for orders. Clerke sent word that King was to warn the natives that Cook's body must be returned the next day or he would destroy the whole village.

Cook's body had been cut in pieces and taken inland, but two high-ranking priests brought part of it back the next day. They were badly frightened men and seemed sincerely to regret what had happened, still believing Cook to be a god. When, they asked, would Lono come again? What would he do to the island people on his return?

The ships remained in the bay for five more days, while the work of stepping the foremast went ahead. During that time more of Cook's broken body was returned, the last of it by one of Terreeoboo's sons, who declared the old king's deep wish for peace. He told Clerke that six leading chiefs, some of them good friends of the white men, had been killed in the fighting and said that the *Discovery*'s boat had been stolen by Pareea's people and broken in pieces, in revenge for the attempt to seize his canoe. Clerke told him to order the whole bay tabooed through the next day, because Cook would be buried during the afternoon.

The ships sailed from Hawaii the day after Cook's burial, setting a course northward to the Kamchatka peninsula on the Asiatic coast opposite Alaska. Here they called at the Russian settlement of Petropavlovsk, where they were warmly welcomed and Clerke had a chance to send word of Cook's death back to England. From Kamchatka they followed the Asiatic coast-line northward to renew their search for the northwest passage. Off northern Siberia they were forced eastward by the solid ice-pack and gradually worked round to the same point they had reached the previous year, off Icy Cape. By this time they were an exhausted and discouraged group of men. The rigging of the ships was badly worn and the *Discovery* had begun to leak. Clerke and some of his officers believed there might be a way through from Icy Cape to Baffin Bay, but they knew it would be madness to attempt it even if they could find a break in the ice. On July 19 Clerke turned southward on the long voyage back to England. It was to be over a hundred and fifty years before the little Mounted Police vessel, *St. Roch*, would make the first successful passage from east to west across the top of the North American continent.

Before they reached Petropavlovsk on the homeward journey, Captain Clerke died of tuberculosis. Lieutenant Gore took over command of the expedition in *Resolution* and Lieutenant King took command of *Discovery*. One very important thing happened on the voyage home. After leaving Petropavlovsk the ships put in at Macao, in southern China, to refit. There the sailors found the sea-otter skins they had traded from the Indians at Nootka Sound were in tremendous demand. Even odd scraps of fur they had been using for bedding brought a good price. Several men made as much as five hundred dollars apiece and more than $10,000 was divided among the crews. The men immediately wanted to sail back to Nootka and for a few days Lieutenant Gore was faced with something approaching mutiny. A few men did desert the ships, to lay the foundations of the fur trade with the Pacific Coast; but the others remained to work them home, knowing they were in no condition to cross the Pacific again, even if the discipline of the Royal Navy had permitted such a venture. They reached England in October of 1780 after a long and difficult voyage, but with all hands in good health.

George Vancouver was now twenty-three years old and had served over eight years at sea. He had sailed round the world once and more than half-way round it again, ranging to within twenty degrees of both the poles. His service had been under a great commander, with first-rate officers and crews. Few naval officers of his time can have had a more thorough or more practical training.

He sat for his examination as lieutenant as soon as he reached London, passed it successfully and was posted to the sloop *Martin*, on channel duty, in December of the same year.

For the next few years it seemed that George Vancouver had settled into the routine service of an active naval officer. The Royal Navy was busy. It was constantly protecting and expanding British interests throughout the Atlantic, the Mediterranean, the Indian Ocean and into the China seas. It was fast growing towards the greatness and glory of Nelson's victories and the power that ruled the seas and maintained peace for a hundred years. Routine service, if it could be called that, was anything but dull, though its difficulties and dangers were very different from those of Cook's great explorations.

Vancouver was not long in the *Martin*. Within a few months he was posted to the 74-gun ship, the *Flame*, of Admiral Rodney's West Indies Squadron, and in 1782 he fought in the great Battle of the Saints, where the French fleet under Admiral de Grasse was completely defeated. The squadron returned to European waters after the battle, but in 1784 Vancouver was posted to the West Indies again, this time under Commodore Alan Gardner. Gardner, knowing his experience and training, set him to making thorough surveys and charts of Port Royal and Kingston Harbour. With Joseph Whidbey, who later sailed as master aboard the *Discovery*, Vancouver did a job that deeply impressed Gardner and led directly to his next posting, which proved to be the most important of his life.

The *Europa* sailed home to England in 1789, just as the Admiralty was preparing a new expedition to the "South Seas and the the Northwest Coast of America". It was the first such expedition since Cook's death and Captain Henry Roberts, the senior midshipman who had been in charge of the pinnace when Cook was killed, was to command it. Vancouver, on the recommendation of Commodore Gardner, was appointed second in command.

No appointment could have pleased Vancouver more. Henry Roberts was a close and valued friend, as well as a fine seaman. There were all the attachments and friendships of the South Seas to be renewed. Above all there was the mystery of that long, rugged, still unexplored northwestern coast-line and the continuing search for the northwest passage. In the years since the last voyage Vancouver had had to listen again and again to contemptuous criticism of Cook's exploration and the blank spots still remaining on his chart of the coast-line. Opinions of fur-traders and adventurers were set against Cook's and believed against his. It was pointed out that he had not found Juan de Fuca's Strait, nor de Fonte's Strait, and had not even followed his own Cook's River to the limit of navigation. To Vancouver, the practical seaman who had known Cook's thoroughness and daring and had experienced the hardships and effort of that voyage, such criticism was infuriating. The chance to share in completing

Cook's work and in proving its soundness filled him with intense satisfaction and stirred his deepest loyalty.

He went at once to supervise the fitting of a new sloop, bought by the Admiralty especially for the voyage and named the *Discovery*. The work went well and by April of 1789 the ship was almost ready to sail. Then there was a sudden threat of war with Spain. British ships had been seized, the flag had been insulted, rights of British subjects had been violated, all in that distant port of Nootka on the northwest coast of America, where Cook's ships had put in and the seamen had traded for sea-otter skins ten years before. The *Discovery*'s supplies were taken for other ships, her crew was scattered through the navy. Captain Roberts went off to the West Indies fleet and Vancouver was posted to the *Courageux* under the command of Sir Alan Gardner. The voyage of exploration, it seemed, was over before it had started.

# 5. Seeds of Dispute

THE dispute at Nootka arose directly out of the visit of the *Resolution* and the old *Discovery* to Macao on the homeward voyage. Seafaring men there, and in other ports around the world, soon knew there was fabulous wealth to be won by trading missions to the unknown northwest coast. There was no shortage of bold and adventurous characters to take up the challenge.

The first of the traders was Captain James Hanna, who sailed from China to Nootka in 1785 and returned the following year with 560 sea-otter skins which sold in China for twenty thousand dollars. He sailed again a month or two later, but by that time half a dozen other ships were in the trade from China, and within the same year Captain Barkley in the *Imperial Eagle* and Captains Dixon and Portlock in the *Queen Charlotte* and *King George* had sailed from London, to reach the coast in 1787.

One of the boldest and most determined of the traders from China was Lieutenant John Meares, recently retired from the Royal Navy, who sailed with the *Nootka* and the *Sea Otter* in 1786. Meares was a good seaman and leader and a fair navigator. He was brave and persistent, but he was also ambitious and unscrupulous.

Meares' first voyage ended in disaster. For some reason, perhaps because he knew of successful Russian trading there, he chose to sail for Prince William Sound. His second ship, the *Sea Otter*, was to meet him in the Sound; but when he arrived she had already left. She was never heard of again. It was already late in the season, so Meares decided to winter in the Sound. Neither his ship nor his crew was equipped for such a winter and before spring twenty-three of his men, including the surgeon, were dead of cold and scurvy. Only Meares, his first officer and one seaman, were strong enough to move around and look after the remaining sick. They, too, would certainly have died in the end had not Captain Dixon arrived in time to give them fresh provisions and lend Meares some of his own men to help work the *Nootka* back to China.

In return for this, Meares agreed to return to China without stopping to trade. But he did trade on his south-ward journey and picked up enough skins to save something of the voyage. Back in China he began at once to raise money for another venture. Early in 1788 he sailed for Nootka with two ships, the *Iphigenia* and the *Felice*.

This time Meares meant to establish himself permanently in the trade. As soon as he arrived at Nootka he bought some land from Chief Maquinna, then set to work to build a trading-post and a small coasting-vessel of about fifty tons, with materials he had brought from China. How much land he bought, what he paid for it and whether he really bought it or just leased it, all became matters of grave and complicated dispute between Britain and Spain later on. But he certainly paid something and received in return some right in the land; and he built a house, with room for men to sleep and work, and laid the keel of his little trading-vessel.

He sailed off southward then in the *Felice,* to trade for furs and search for the mouth of the great river which was later named the Columbia. He found the bay where the river enters the ocean, but was turned back by the breakers without finding the river. He named the bay Deception Bay and its northward point Cape Disappointment, then sailed for Nootka again. On the way he found the entrance to the Strait of Juan de Fuca and sent his long-boat some distance into the strait.

When he reached Nootka he found his little coasting-ship was almost built. On September 20th, 1788, she was launched, the first ship ever built in the Pacific northwest. Maquinna and Callicum, the two great native chiefs, came to the launching, with many of their people. Guns were fired, flags were flown and Captain Gray with the American ship *Washington*, which had just come into the port, helped to celebrate the event. Four days later Meares sailed for China with the *Felice*, leaving Captain Douglas in charge of the settlement. Early in the following year he sent two more ships, the *Princess Royal*, Captain Hudson, and the *Argonaut*, Captain Colnett, to trade for furs out of Nootka.

At about this time the Spaniards in Mexico, who laid claim to sovereignty over all the Pacific coast of North and South America, became suddenly concerned about the activity of British, American and Russian fur-traders. It was true that the Spaniards had no settlement on the coast north of San Francisco, but they still felt they had the only rightful claim to control of the northwest by virtue of a three-hundred-year-old declaration of the Pope, as well as by the voyages of Perez and Hecata and Quadra. So in 1789 they sent Don Estevan Jose Martinez to Nootka with the *Princessa* and the *San Carlos*. His orders were to take possession of the port of Nootka and establish a Spanish settlement there.

When Martinez reached Nootka with his two warships he found Captain Douglas still there with the *Iphigenia* and an American ship, the *Columbia,* also in the port. The *Northwest America* was away on a trading cruise farther up the coast.

Martinez entered the port and took charge of it as Spanish territory. Captain Douglas and Captain Kendrick of the *Columbia* accepted this, as they were bound to in the face of the Spanish guns, and at first things went quite smoothly. But the *Iphigenia* was flying Portuguese colours and sailing under Portuguese orders, to evade the trading monopoly of the East India Company. Martinez objected to certain clauses in the sailing orders, arrested Douglas and seized the ship. After about ten days he released the ship, with orders to return straight to China. Douglas sailed out of the port readily enough, but made a successful trading cruise before going back to China with word of what was happening at Nootka.

Early in June the *Northwest America* came back to Nootka. Martinez seized her at once, struck the British colours and hoisted the Spanish flag. A week later Captain Hudson came in from China with the *Princess Royal*. Martinez allowed him to take on wood and water and leave the port. As Hudson left, Colnett came in with the

*Argonaut*. He was suspicious and not at all inclined to accept Spanish domination, but Martinez promised not to molest his ship, so he entered the port. When he was ready to sail Martinez demanded his sailing orders and other details of the ship's commission. Colnett angrily refused and was immediately arrested. When Hudson came back to look for him, he also was arrested. Spanish crews were put aboard the *Princess Royal* and the *Argonaut* and Martinez sent both ships down to the Spanish port of San Blas as prizes.

First word of all this reached London early in 1790. Notes began to pass between the British and Spanish governments. At first the Spaniards tried to brush aside all protests and insist on their claim to full sovereignty over the whole Pacific Coast of America. But British power was growing and the British people were in no mood to accept an insult to the flag or any restriction of their rights at sea. In April John Meares arrived in England and gave his own highly coloured version of the story to King and Parliament. Parliament immediately voted a million pounds to assemble and equip a powerful fleet. Roberts and Vancouver returned to regular naval duty and the newly fitted *Discovery* lay at her moorings in the Thames.

War threatened through most of 1790 and the fleet patrolled the seas, ready for action. But in the end, the Spanish government signed the Nootka Convention, which ensured the British equal access for purposes of trade and settlement to all the western coast of North America lying northward of the established Spanish settlements in California. Meares and his partners were handsomely compensated and their ships were returned. The Convention also provided that all lands at Nootka occupied by Meares should be returned to Britain.

The voyage planned for the *Discovery* was now more important than ever. Since Captain Roberts was still away in the West Indies, George Vancouver was promoted to the rank of Commander and given charge of the expedition, which included the armed tender *Chatham*, under Lieutenant William Broughton. In addition to his orders to explore the whole northwest coast of America, from latitude 30°N. in California to 60°N. in Alaska, and to search thoroughly for a northwest passage, Vancouver was made the King's Commissioner, with power to receive back the lands at Nootka. He was to expect further orders by the supply ship *Daedalus*, which would serve the expedition from the new British colony in Australia.

# 6. The Great Voyage Starts

DISCOVERY and *Chatham* sailed from Falmouth on April 1st, 1791. The great voyage had begun and, though Vancouver sincerely regretted that his friend, Roberts, was not with him, he was a proud and confident commander. Everything in nineteen years of sea experience and training ideally fitted him for this command. He was going into dangerous and little-known waters, but no man in the world knew more of them than he did; he would be completing the work of the commander whose memory he revered and at the same time helping to defend that great man, Captain Cook, from his detractors. He had hand-picked officers and crews, men like Joseph Whidbey who had served under him as master in the West Indies and Peter Puget who had been a midshipman aboard Commodore Gardner's flagship; like Zachary Mudge, his tough senior lieutenant, and brilliant young Spelman Swaine, the master's mate. Aboard the *Chatham* he had sturdy, dependable Broughton as commander, and brave, persistent James Johnstone as master, men as devoted as he was himself to the causes of the voyage.

The ships were well equipped. The Admiralty had refused nothing and skimped on nothing and Vancouver himself had known exactly what to ask for. But in spite of all the careful preparations it quickly became clear that the expedition had a serious weakness: the *Chatham* was a cranky, awkward little ship and a poor sailer in any wind. Even before they left the English Channel Vancouver had sent most of the *Discovery*'s heavy shot aboard her for extra ballast. This made her reasonably safe to handle, but she was still very slow and Johnstone commented bitterly that, small as she was, she drew twelve and a half feet of water and was utterly unsuited for exploring rivers and shallow places. The *Chatham* was a ship of 120 tons, manned by a crew of 45; the *Discovery*, 330 tons, just under a hundred feet long and with a crew of 100 men, drew only fifteen feet of water.

The two ships, with the *Discovery* carrying easy sail and holding back to wait for her consort, made a good passage to the Cape of Good Hope, arriving on July 9th. There they stopped for about a month, to take water and fresh provisions and refit, for Vancouver knew it would be a long while before they could hope to put in at another civilized port. From there he sailed towards the southwest coast of Australia, which was still a blank space on the maps of the world, supposed rather than known to exist. Land was sighted from the masthead on September 26th, about six weeks after leaving the Cape. The ships moved in close next day and Vancouver named Cape Howe, the southwest corner of the continent. Before noon *Chatham* led the way into a safe harbour, which was named King George the Third's Sound.

Vancouver was closely following the pattern of Cook's voyages. He had to guard the health of his crews and keep his ships in condition for the hard service of the main part

RUSSIA

NORTH AMERICA

EXPLORATIONS
of
NORTH-WEST COAST
of
AMERICA

MONTEREY

HAWAIIAN
ISLANDS

COCOS Is.
GALAPAGOS
ISLANDS

AUSTRALIA

SOCIETY ISLANDS

JUAN
FERNAN
ISLAN

NEW ZEALAND

MAP OF THE WORLD
*showing*
CAPTAIN VANCOUVER'S VOYAGE
1791—1795

of the voyage; but he had Cook's instinct for exploration and discovery in full measure and he was determined to miss no opportunity that could be fitted in with these main duties. The long voyage from England had not been without loss. As they left the Channel, John Brown, the carpenter's mate and an important man, had been lost overboard. Four men whose health was not strong enough for the voyage had been sent home from the Cape. Leaving the Cape, *Discovery*'s crew had suffered an epidemic of dysentery and one of the marines, Neil Coil, had died of it. Cranston, the surgeon, had been very sick, but Archibald Menzies, the expedition's botanist who was also a surgeon, had been able to take over his duties. Twenty or more of the crew had been close to death and were still too weak to work when the ships reached Australia. It was a good opportunity to rest them and for two weeks the ships remained in the Sound, exploring it thoroughly.

They found a strange land, quiet and deserted, yet with signs that humans lived there. Trees and brush on some of the forested slopes had been burned; primitive fish weirs had been built in the streams; all the birds and animals were shy and wild. At two places on the Sound were collections of simple brush shelters that showed signs of recent habitation. But none of the natives was seen.

The ship's crews caught mullet and other fish and found a wonderful bed of oysters that gave them several good meals. They were less successful in hunting the wild-fowl and the handsome black swans, which were numerous but wild. On the land they found wild celery and other vegetables and gumwood for fuel, while Menzies collected many new plants. Vancouver took formal possession of the Sound and the coast-line extending from it in the name of the King.

When the ships left the Sound in the middle of October the crews were rested and refreshed and the convalescents were recovering well. For a full month they sailed along the southern coast-line of Australia, naming the headlands and other prominent features, plotting them on to the charts until the unknown, empty space gradually took shape. It was an inhospitable coast, with few harbours. Violent gales from the south were a constant threat, forcing the ships to hold well off the land. Still short-handed, because the sick men had not recovered strength, Vancouver decided that the risk to his ships was too great and set a course for Dusky Bay in New Zealand.

In Dusky Bay, while his men cut timber, brewed spruce beer, caught fish and shot wild-fowl, Vancouver took stock and made his plans. It was November of 1790, and he was nearly eight months out from England. His ships were in good shape and his men were rapidly renewing their health in the summer weather, on the good supplies the bay afforded. It would be April before the weather would be good enough for work on the northwest coast of of America. Meanwhile he had ten thousand miles of ocean sailing ahead of him and a call to make at the Hawaiian Islands to leave Toweroo, a native Hawaiian who had been taken to England by the ship *Prince of Wales* two years earlier. Four full months was plenty of time for all this and Vancouver's happy memories of Tahiti suggested to him that he might very well do his main provisioning and repairs there. Tahiti was also the ideal place to check his chronometers and other navigation instruments, because its position was exactly known.

This was the fifth time Vancouver had anchored in Dusky Bay. Shortly after the ships arrived there they were hit by the most violent storm he had seen in all his years at sea. The skies blackened and lightning flashed over the hills. In spite of the shelter of the harbour, seas broke clear over the *Chatham* as she rode at anchor. *Discovery* struck her top-masts and put out all her spare anchors, but for hours she was in danger of being smashed to pieces in the pounding surf only forty yards away. Yet Vancouver found it a good place to be, generous to all the needs of his ships and his men. He was not a sentimental man, but he remembered that this was the first unexplored harbour he had known. He remembered it as the entrance to all the mysteries of the wide Pacific; to Tahiti, where he could hope to see his old friend Otoo again; to the Hawaiian Islands, where Cook was buried and where other native friends would some day try to explain how he had died; to the challenge of the unexplored American coast-line, where his present duty lay. When he gave Broughton sailing orders for Matavai Bay in Tahiti and the ships put to sea again it was, in a very real sense, the true start of the great voyage.

Almost as they left the bay, the two ships ran into another fierce storm. There was nothing they could do but run southward to get as far as possible away from the dangers of the land. Through the remaining daylight they kept together, though often hidden from each other by driving spray and the enormous waves. But as night fell they quickly became separated, in spite of flares and gun-shots.

As she rode on into the storm with her topgallant masts struck and her topsails reefed, *Discovery* seemed to become heavier and slower and harder to handle. Suspecting a leak, Vancouver ordered the pumps manned, but they sucked no water. The ship wallowed more and more clumsily and Vancouver began to worry about the little cluster of rocky

48

islets to the south of New Zealand, which Cook had named the Snares. He ordered the carpenter below to check the holds. The man came back, white-faced and shaken. There was six feet of water in the holds and the pumps were clogged. Quietly Vancouver ordered them cleared and rode his ship as easily as he could into the shattering swells. Like Cook, he felt danger at sea only as a challenge, to be met by seamanship and a calm mind. But he knew that there could be little hope for his ship or his people unless the pumps could keep pace with the leak.

Word came back more quickly than he had dared hope. The pumps were gaining fast. They had been clogged for a long while, perhaps all through the stay in Dusky Bay, and the ship had no serious leaks. Within a few hours the holds were dry and the ship rode easily, though the storm raged as fiercely as ever. With no hope of finding the *Chatham* until she should come safely to Tahiti, Vancouver held well southward to clear the Snares, then set a course northeastward, still riding the gale, for Matavai Bay.

In time the storm blew out and the *Discovery* rode the Pacific on fair winds, cutting a track at a distance from Cook's to explore new water. So she came upon the tiny undiscovered island of Rapa, standing like a white sail in the wide Pacific. Vancouver hove to, to talk with the natives who came off in canoes and fix the position of the island. But he made no attempt to anchor or send a boat ashore because the wind was fair and he was anxious to reach Tahiti and find the *Chatham*. A week later, on December 30th, they came in sight of Matavai Bay and were met by great numbers of natives in canoes. Another ship, they said, had arrived a few days earlier and was safely anchored in the bay.

# 7. Tahiti

BROUGHTON in the *Chatham* did his best to follow *Discovery* into the storm. But the *Chatham* was a wet little ship; she ploughed into the waves instead of rising to them and tons of water crashed over her and down upon her decks, threatening the rigging, tearing loose the barrels and casks that were lashed down and floating them to pound against masts and bulwarks. The jolly-boat was battered to pieces and the seamen could move to their work only at greatest hazard. In the end Broughton snugged down to a reefed trysail and a fore-staysail and brought his ship into the wind to ride out the gale. By the time the storm was over he had been carried far to the southward and eastward and his course for Tahiti took him on a line well over from *Discovery*'s.

They ran into bad weather again, with following seas that swept over the ship from astern; but Broughton was able to run before it. When the weather cleared they were in sight of land, though the charts showed only an empty ocean. The land proved to be a group of islands, which Broughton named the Chatham Islands after his ship. He worked the ship as close as he could, then launched a small boat and went in with Johnstone, the master, and Sheriff, the master's mate, to explore his discovery and take possession of it.

Broughton's purpose was to learn whether the islands were useful—if they would provide safe anchorage, supplies and fresh water for ships, and whether the natives were friendly or hostile. He took the boat into a sheltered bay with a good sandy beach, where some natives had been seen from the ship. A few canoes were drawn up on the rocks just inside the bay and the party landed to examine them, finding fish nets and broad hardwood paddles skilfully and intelligently made, though the only signs of a village were a few simple brush shelters back among the trees.

While they were still examining the canoes, a group of forty or fifty natives came along the beach towards them. Broughton ordered his people back into the boat and waited for the natives to come up. They came quite boldly, talking excitedly, pointing to the sun and asking by signs if the white men had come down from it. Broughton gave them a few beads and trinkets and they signed for the party to come ashore and visit their huts. They were well armed with spears and clubs, but Sheriff laid down his musket and cutlass and went ashore alone. They took him by the hands to pull him towards the huts and signalled that they wanted to keep him. But Sheriff managed to make it clear that he did not want to go, even though he was their friend; so they released him and let him go back to the boat.

Broughton was unable to decide whether they were friendly or dangerous. Others had come up now, also armed with spears and clubs, and they were so numerous that he decided against risking a landing. But he still wanted to learn more about the island, especially whether it had a good supply of fresh water, so he took the boat across to the other side of the bay. The natives were there before them, but they were fewer and seemed less hostile, so Broughton landed with Johnstone and three armed seamen, leaving Sheriff to follow in the boat with four more men. Broughton shook hands and rubbed noses with a few of the natives, gave them more trinkets and tried to explain that he wanted fresh water. They seemed not to understand, so he began walking along the beach towards where he had seen something like an inland lake from the ship. The natives followed and Broughton and Johnstone noticed that those who had no spears were picking up driftwood clubs from the beach.

Suddenly, and for no apparent reason, they became obviously hostile. One young brave stamped his feet, strutted insultingly and made faces. Broughton pointed his gun at him and shouted to Sheriff to pull in with the boat. As the boat turned, the natives closed in. Broughton fired a load of bird-shot, hoping to scare off the attack, but a vicious blow from a club knocked Johnstone's gun out of his hand. He snatched it up again and fired at once. A marine and a seaman, forced into the water, also fired in self-defence, without orders. Then another shot came from the boat and the natives ran. For a moment Broughton hoped it was a bloodless victory. Then he saw a man lying on the beach and found that a bullet had smashed through his arm and into his heart.

Soberly, he continued his brief exploration of the island, then left some presents in the deserted canoes to make what amends he could for the injury that had been done. The natives had laughed and joked with his men and had seemed a cheerful, good-natured people until their sudden show of hostility. He regretted the wasted death, as he knew Vancouver would when he heard of it. But it was one of the risks of exploration that would be met many times in the course of the voyage, and at least his own crew had escaped death or injury.

The *Chatham* sailed from the islands that evening and made an uneventful passage to Tahiti, arriving at Matavai Bay shortly before the *Discovery*.

There was a great deal to be done at Tahiti and Vancouver set about it at once. Soon the carpenters were whipsawing the Dusky Bay logs into planks and getting ready to build a replacement for the *Chatham*'s jolly-boat. All the sails were unbent on both ships, the top-masts were struck and rigging was completely overhauled. An observatory was set up on shore under a guard of marines and the chronometers and other instruments were closely and constantly checked.

The natives were friendly and it was an ideal chance to trade for fresh provisions. To maintain the full value of the trade goods, private trading by members of the crews was forbidden; but there was very little difficulty, because the natives were now accustomed to European articles and traded eagerly for them. Vancouver saw with regret that they had lost many of their primitive skills and crafts and would be left almost helpless without regular supplies of iron and cloth, as well as hatchets and other tools. He was careful to report later to the Admiralty that since Euro-

peans had created these needs they were bound by all the laws of humanity to see that regular supplies were sent out to the islands.

There were many other changes in the islands which distressed him, for Vancouver had a deep and sincere affection for all the simple native races and, like Cook, a great skill in winning their trust and friendship. But he found his old friend King Otoo, whom he had known as a shy and uncertain young man in his thirties, had grown immensely in power and wisdom and dignity. He was no longer called Otoo, but Pomurrey, because he had already withdrawn from formal sovereignty in favour of his eldest son, a boy of nine, who had taken the name Otoo. Young Otoo was treated with enormous respect by all the people including his father. He went everywhere surrounded by a picked bodyguard and was usually carried on the shoulders of one of them. Every move he made was governed by ceremony and the most rigid taboos; any cup or dish he drank from had to be instantly broken and he could not go aboard the ships because any dwelling he entered had to be destroyed as soon as he left it.

But Pomurrey still held the real power in an easy, natural way, as though guarding it for his son during the period of initiation and training. Vancouver and Broughton had to pay their most formal respects to Otoo and ask through him for everything they wanted. But Pomurrey gave the orders and saw that they were carried out, and Pomurrey proved himself a real friend in every way. Both he and Mahow, a very old man who was his prime minister, stayed aboard the *Discovery* with their wives as long as she was anchored in the bay.

Relieved of the formal duties of kingship and sure of his

power, Pomurrey had become a very relaxed man, who liked nothing better than a good time. He and Mahow ate regularly at Vancouver's table and Pomurrey soon found that brandy had a delightful effect upon him. One evening after supper he took a whole bottle and drank it straight down. The effect was a little too much. He became sick, then violent and it took four men to hold him down and quiet him. After that he slept for an hour and awoke feeling fine. He at once asked for more brandy.

Vancouver tried to talk him out of it, explaining its ill effects. But Pomurrey would have none of that. Vancouver, he said, was not "tio tio"—not a good sport. Vancouver considered this carefully and with some amusement. He valued Pomurrey's friendship highly and did not want to risk anything that would injure his health; but he decided Pomurrey was strong enough to stand almost anything and wise enough to learn from experience, so he gave orders he was to have all the brandy he wanted. Within a week Pomurrey had learned. He would take no more than a glass of wine at dinner. Vancouver, he said, was quite right. Brandy did bad things to men and he wanted no more of it.

If Pomurrey seems rather a simple man in this affair, it was because he was dealing with an unfamiliar thing. In all other matters both he and Mahow were highly intelligent and their power among the islanders was firmly based on skill in war and government. Both men followed all Vancouver's work with the keenest interest and helped him in every possible way. Old Mahow, who was dying, had himself carried everywhere on a litter, to watch the sawing of planks, the building and repair of boats and all the other work that was going on. Both men closely watched the work at the observatory and tried to understand the sighting of the sun and the accurate performance of the chronometers.

Vancouver, for his part, found real pleasure in their company and never tired of discussing with them all the details of island politics, the methods of warfare and agriculture and anything that had to do with the welfare of the island people. He wanted their friendship not only for himself, but for any European ships that might visit the islands after him.

Shortly before the ships were due to leave, old Mahow died. Pomurrey and all the people showed the greatest evidence of respect and grief for the old man. The mourning period lasted for several days and through the whole time no fires were lighted, no canoes moved from shore and there was no travel over the island trails. The funeral ceremonies were complicated and often very secret. The old man's body was taken away to the hills at first and then brought back in a succession of ceremonies. Sometimes Vancouver and Menzies were invited to attend, sometimes they were forbidden. Menzies was particularly anxious to see as much as possible, because the islanders were believed to have some embalming secrets unknown to white men. But Pomurrey's orders were always strictly obeyed and he was unable to learn what these were, though he saw Mahow's corpse in excellent preservation several days after his death.

Gradually life returned to normal. The work of the ships was almost done, but at the last moment it was found that the Hawaiian islander, Toweroo, was missing—he had fallen in love with a chief's daughter and run off into the hills with her. Besides this, a number of axes and "Mr.

Broughton's linen", which presumably means his spare shirts and underwear, were stolen. Vancouver at once seized a chief he suspected, but Pomurrey assured him that the man was innocent and promised to bring back Toweroo and everything that was missing. In a few days Toweroo was found and brought back and the axes were returned. But Mr. Broughton's linen was not. It was an irreplaceable loss under those conditions and Vancouver scolded Pomurrey for the bad faith of his people and refused the fireworks display he had promised them, which was a serious disappointment to a people so fond of fun and merry-making. But the linen was still not found and in the end Vancouver realized it was beyond Pomurrey's power to get it, perhaps because it had been cut up for other uses.

Vancouver was torn between his friendship for Pomurrey and his determination to teach the natives to deal honestly with ships that came in to trade. He would not relent about the fireworks, to Pomurrey's disappointment. But they parted in friendship and respect and Vancouver held to his opinion of Pomurrey as a great and wise chief and a true friend.

# 8. Juan de Fuca Strait

THE ships reached the Hawaiian Islands, or the Sandwich Islands as Cook and Vancouver called them, in seven weeks of steady sailing over a distance of 2,400 miles.

The islands were of great importance to the expedition, because Vancouver intended to use them as a wintering base during the two or three years he expected to spend in his exploration of the American coast-line. But he found them now in a state of confusion from tribal wars that had been going on since the death of the old king Terreeoboo some years before. It was difficult to learn which chiefs were in authority and the people, though not actively hostile, were unfriendly and unhelpful. He was disappointed, too, in his hope of meeting his supply ship, the *Daedalus*, there. He was able to leave Toweroo safely ashore under the protection of Tianna, an important chief in the Island of Hawaii; and he took on a good supply of fresh water at Kauai. But there was nothing else to be done at that time and the ships sailed for the North American coast in the middle of March.

George Vancouver was now thirty-five years old. He was a heavily-built man of moderate height, with a fair complexion and grey eyes, strongly flecked with yellow. His face was fleshy, with a double chin, a long straight nose and a firm, rather thin-lipped mouth; his thick eyebrows arched sharply to a broad straight forehead under a short powdered wig. It was a confident face, with the calm, religious certainty of his Dutch ancestors strongly in it. He looked still a young man, which he was, even though his friend Pomurrey had been shocked by the change in him. He looked well, which he was not; Menzies was already paying particular attention to his health and prescribing for the cough and chest pains that sometimes bothered him.

By all normal standards, Vancouver was a very lonely man. Practically his whole life had been spent at sea and he had had little chance to make friends except among his shipmates. Now he was older than any of his officers and sharply separated from them by the necessities of command. He should have made a friend of Menzies, but could not, partly because his commanding, aggressive character differed sharply from that of the gentle naturalist, partly because he resented Menzies' rather independent position under his command. Menzies was as devoted to his job as Vancouver was to his, and just as determined about it, so the two men were often at cross-purposes when they should have been in closest agreement. Vancouver had an affection for his sisters and a deep love of his brother John in England, whom he had seen all too seldom since going to sea; but apart from this the ruling factor of his life was the memory and example of Cook, which he kept constantly before him.

60

It was before him now, as he sailed from the scene of Cook's death towards the work Cook had left unfinished, and he was not lonely. He loved the sturdy ship he commanded and the towering reach of her canvas that sighed and sang above him. He was happy in his officers, in their keenness for the work ahead and their sure and steady performance of every duty asked of them; he loved his people, the rough and simple seamen who served under him, each with his own skills, his own faults, his own capacity for bearing the hardships and answering the demands of service.

As the ships neared the North American coast he spent more and more time with the charts in his cabin, planning the work he had already planned a hundred times. There were Cook's charts, in some of which he himself had had a hand, charts made by Captains Portlock and Dixon and other fur-traders, Spanish charts; there were charts that showed great rivers and imaginary inland seas, charts that showed the Straits of Juan de Fuca, the Straits of de Fonte, the Straits of Anian, all openings in the land that might or might not lead to the northwest passage. But the one that drew his attention again and again was a map drawn by John Meares which showed the track of the American sloop *Lady Washington*, commanded by Captain Gray, in 1789.

Vancouver knew Meares had travelled the coast extensively and had sent one of his boats a considerable distance into the Strait of Juan de Fuca. His map showed that the *Lady Washington* had entered an inland sea north of the Queen Charlotte Islands and followed it down to come out to the Pacific again by the Strait of Juan de Fuca, five hundred miles to the southward. Like other seamen of his time, Vancouver had the gravest doubts of Meares' truthfulness. But this mysterious track, at least a hundred miles *inside* the track of Cook's ships along the coast-line, stirred his imagination. He was determined to prove it or disprove it by following every turn and twist of the continental shore-line to its last limits. Where the ships could not go, small boats would, no matter what the cost in time and hardship and courage. That, he knew, was the nearest measure he could find of the task ahead, and he would not turn his ships for England again until the measure was met.

The ships sighted the North American coast on April 17, 1792, at latitude $39°17'$, about a hundred miles north of San Francisco. From that point Vancouver began his survey. At first it was a fairly simple matter of keeping the land in sight through each day's sailing, holding off at night, then turning in again at dawn to pick up the last landmark of the previous night and follow on from there.

The coast-line generally was what Vancouver called "compact"—that is to say, it ran quite evenly, without noticeable bays or inlets or other indentations. Often there were low cliffs, sometimes sandy beaches with breakers in front of them. It was not a coast that ships could approach too closely except under ideal weather conditions. But it seemed easy to chart it most accurately without going so close as to endanger the ships.

This led Vancouver into the first great error of his voyage. He came to the point Meares had named Cape Disappointment and recognized the bay to the south of it as Deception Bay, which Meares had also named. He knew that Meares had come there in search of the mouth of a great river that was shown on the Spanish charts and had decided, after turning back from the breakers, that "no

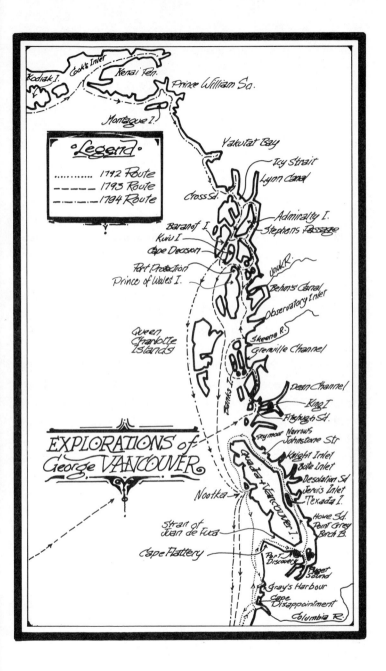

EXPLORATIONS of George VANCOUVER

Legend
.......... 1792 Route
 1793 Route
··· 1794 Route

Kodiak I.
Cook's Inlet
Kenai Pen.
Prince William So.
Montague I.
Yakutat Bay
Icy Strait
Lynn Canal
Cross Sd.
Admiralty I.
Baranof I.
Stephens Passage
Kuiu I.
Cape Decision
Port Protection
Prince of Wales I.
Unuk R.
Behm's Canal
Observatory Inlet
Queen Charlotte Islands
Skeena R.
Grenville Channel
Banks I.
Dean Channel
King I.
Fitzhugh's Sd.
Seymour Narrows
Johnstone Str.
Knight Inlet
Bute Inlet
Desolation Sd.
Jervis Inlet
Texada I.
Nootka
Island Vancouver I.
Howe Sd.
Point Grey
Birch B.
Strait of Juan de Fuca
Cape Flattery
Port Discovery
Puget Sound
Gray's Harbour
Cape Disappointment
Columbia R.

such river exists". But Vancouver could see that the salt water had changed from its natural blue to the silt-laden grey of river water and that the land behind Deception Bay was flat and low. Every sign of a great river was there —even the breakers were a sign not just of shallow water, but of the powerful river current meeting the ocean swells. And the ships were off the mouth of the bay through the better part of a day in fair weather.

All this was discussed on board *Discovery* and Menzies even climbed to the masthead and saw what seemed to him a river or an inlet going in on the south side of Cape Disappointment. All Vancouver had to do was anchor his ships and send his small boats in to explore, as he did again and again throughout the rest of the voyage. But his mind was on the Strait of Juan de Fuca. The wind was fair and he could hope to reach it in two days' sailing time or less. The river-coloured water, he decided, was merely the flow of several small streams coming out through the low-lying land. So the ships held on their course up the coast, leaving the mouth of the Columbia River to be discovered just two weeks later when the American fur-trader, Captain Gray, sailed his ship successfully through the breakers that had turned Meares back and warned Vancouver away.

*Discovery* and *Chatham* met Gray's ship, the *Columbia*, just outside the Strait of Juan de Fuca two days later. Vancouver asked Gray to stop his ship and sent Lieutenant Puget and Mr. Menzies over to ask him about the voyage through the inland sea shown on Meares' chart. Gray told them very plainly that he knew nothing at all of the voyage he was supposed to have made in the *Lady Washington*; he had sailed about fifty miles into the strait and had come out by the same way, though the natives had told him that the opening extended a long distance to the northward.

Vancouver was delighted by the news. He could be sure now that no one had probed to the limits of Juan de Fuca Strait and no one had tested the theory that Nootka and other west coast ports were on islands rather than the mainland of the continent. The work he had brought his ships round the world to do was still waiting to be done, and it promised to be even more exciting and worth while than he had expected.

# 9. From Port Discovery

VANCOUVER met Gray in the *Columbia* on the morning of Sunday, 29th April, 1792. That same evening he rounded Cape Flattery and sailed into the Strait of Juan de Fuca on a fresh southeast gale. It was raining and the weather was hazy, so there was little to be seen; but as the ships sailed up the strait the high mountains of the Olympic peninsula cut off the full strength of the gale and they anchored for the night about eight miles from the entrance, near the southern shore.

The next day was clear and sunny, with a gentle breeze from the northwest. The deep-sea men and the deep-sea ships were sailing now with land on both sides of them. No one knew what lay ahead and very few among them could have guessed it would be more than three months before they would see the open ocean again. Vancouver stood on his quarter-deck, watching the shore-lines. To the south were low, sandy cliffs dropping down to beaches of sand or stones. Behind the cliffs the land climbed gently through dark evergreen forests until the hills suddenly became the great shining mountains of the Olympic range, rock-walled and crowned with snow. Twenty miles away, on the other side of the strait, the San Juan hills were gentler and more rounded, with the timber holding almost to their tops and far less snow on the heights. Ahead, to the east, the strait was blue in the sunlight, ruffled by the light westerly, seemingly endless. This was the way to the inland sea that the old Greek pilot, Juan de Fuca, claimed to have entered and sailed in for twenty days exactly two hundred years earlier. It might still be the way, as had been claimed so often since that time, to a northwest passage and the reward of £20,000 promised by the British government for its discovery; it might be the inland waterway northward that Meares had shown on his map; or it could be the way to any of a hundred other new and exciting things.

George Vancouver welcomed the task ahead, whatever it might be, and he knew that his people were ready for it. He would not turn back from the inland sea, no matter where it led him, until he had searched out its last recess and solved its ultimate secret. All that day the ships sailed on up the strait in pleasant weather and late in the afternoon Joseph Baker, the third lieutenant of the *Discovery*, sighted the peak of a craggy mountain dead ahead. By evening the mountain itself was in plain sight, an enormous snow-piled mass, towering above the other peaks, its base hidden in clouds over the flat land that made the eastern shore of the inland sea.

The ships anchored for the night behind a long, low, sandy spit that reminded Vancouver of Dungeness in the English Channel, and he named it New Dungeness. The next day was as bright and lovely as the day before. Everyone aboard both ships was excited by the beauty of the land they had come to and the prospect of new discovery everywhere in sight. To the eastward the broad sweep of the strait was broken by islands. Towards the north the scattered islands seemed only to promise a choice of channels leading back into the mainland far beyond them. On every side were green, timbered slopes climbing away to the white peaks of the moutains, where a winter's snow lay smooth and deep.

The ships needed a fully protected anchorage, near good supplies of wood and water, so Vancouver and Menzies and several of the officers went off in three of the small boats with a day's provisions, on what may well have been the first real picnic on the northwest coast. They rowed along close to shore, starting up flight after flight of ducks and geese that were resting on their northward migration. Several shotguns were aboard and the sportsmen of the expedition fired often, though with little success because the birds were wild and the flocks always rose well wide of the boats. The first bay they came to was closed off by a narrow sand-spit across its entrance, so they held on to a small island in the mouth of the next bay. Here they went eagerly ashore, to feel solid ground and stretch their legs for the first time after six long weeks aboard the ships.

The island, which was later named Protection Island, was guarded by steep sand cliffs on the northwest side; but they climbed a long grassy slope from the south to a wide meadow, covered with grass and clover and wild-flowers in bloom. A few great Douglas firs with heavy, spreading limbs were scattered about the meadow and on the north side, along the top of the cliffs, was a solid belt of big trees

68

and heavy brush that gave shelter from the breeze. Menzies delightedly examined everything, exclaiming over wild gooseberries and wild roses just in bloom, stopping again and again to admire great glowing clumps of sea blush. From the high level of the meadow they could see the blue water sparkling away to north and east, spreading between the islands, cutting deeply into the land in long arms and inlets that seemed to welcome exploration.

From this island they took the boats on into the arm behind it, finding a sheltered harbour, good beaches, deep anchorage and abundant timber —everything they needed except a good supply of fresh water. Then Vancouver in the yawl came upon a strong-flowing stream. They went ashore there and built a fire and made their meal. It was midnight before they got back to the ships again, but they were a happy group of men, full of the pleasures of the day and eager to begin exploration of the lovely land they had found.

Next day the ships moved up to the new anchorage, which Vancouver named Port Discovery. The weather was still perfect and everyone went to work at once. The observatory was set up and the instruments were sent ashore: gunners aired powder, sail-makers worked on the sails, riggers swarmed all over both ships while carpenters caulked the leaky decks and sides; parties of seamen went ashore to cut wood and brew spruce beer; coopers checked the water and provision casks and got them ready for fresh supplies. By Sunday, May 6th, everything was going so well that Vancouver declared the first full holiday the men had had since leaving the Cape of Good Hope.

That same evening he ordered the *Chatham*'s cutter

and *Discovery's* yawl and launch to be armed and provisioned for a five-day journey, and at daylight next morning they started on the first of innumerable small boat explorations. Vancouver himself went in the yawl, with Menzies and two midshipmen; Puget commanded the launch and Johnstone the cutter. Broughton was left in charge of the ships and the work that was still to be done in them; Whidbey was responsible for the work ashore in the observatory and for the detailed survey of Port Discovery.

The small boats were essentially the scouts of the expedition. It was Vancouver's intention to follow out the whole length of the continental shore-line from latitude 30°N. to 60°N., tracing it through every possible confusion of islands, following every branch and arm and inlet to its ultimate end, leaving no remotest possibility of a northwest passage untested. With this intention he gave the order that the boats were to keep the shore-line always in sight on the starboard or right-hand side, no matter where it led them. He had done this successfully with his ships from California northward, missing only the Columbia and the breaker-ridden entrances of Willapa Bay and Gray's Harbour. But now the way was too tortuous and uncertain for the ships.

The small boats were no more than twenty feet long, quite stoutly built and designed to carry a good quantity of supplies and other equipment. The smallest of them was the *Chatham's* jolly-boat, a clinker-built row-boat used for minor jobs such as ferrying light loads of men and supplies to and from shore; she was never sent off on the long explorations. The cutters were somewhat larger and broad enough for two oarsmen to sit side by side. The launch was the largest of the boats with room for ten oars. Vancouver's favourite, the yawl, was rowed by six oars and carried two square lug-sails and a fore-sail, the mizzen projecting outboard over the stern as it does in a modern yawl. She was about eighteen feet long and like the other boats, without decking or cabin or any protection from the weather except a canvas awning.

The first trip of the small boats led them at once into another deep bay which Vancouver named Port Townshend, after the man who had taken over command from the dying General Wolfe at Quebec. Near the head of the bay they came upon a recently deserted Indian village and were shocked to find several human heads impaled on stakes, as well as charred human bones in the embers of a fire. It was clearly the result of some recent local war or raid, but it was also a warning to them not to trust the Indians too far in spite of the friendliness of those who had visited the ships since they entered the strait. From Port Townshend they also had first sight of a round, massive, snowy mountain, some way south of Mount Baker, which Vancouver named Rainier after his friend Rear-Admiral Rainier.

Beyond Port Townshend the shore-line led them into a long, narrow, twisting inlet that took several days to explore and was the first real test of Vancouver's method. It was also the first hint of the exhausting and immensely difficult work ahead. Hood Canal, which was the name given to the long inlet, is over sixty miles from Foulweather Bluff at its entrance to Lynch Cove at its head; another narrow bay runs back from it for over ten miles. So the boats travelled nearly a hundred and fifty miles to trace this single stretch of continental shore-line, almost entirely by rowing, often against strong tides and unfavourable winds. Through most of this journey the weather was clear and fine. The Indians they met were friendly and willingly traded salmon and flounders and clams. Nothing held them up or slowed them unduly. But by the time they reached the head of the canal and turned back they were already six days away from the ships, with provisions almost exhausted.

Off Foulweather Bluff on the return journey they ran into heavy rain and a rough easterly wind. When they reached the ships in Port Discovery at three in the afternoon on May 15th they were wet and hungry and exhausted. The old dull food and the uncomfortable quarters looked very good to them. Menzies settled down to record and classify the many wonderful things he had seen—sand-hill cranes and red-wing blackbirds, oriental arbutus trees, broad-leaf maples, oak and cascara and hazel-nut trees, the skin of a great mountain lion worn by one of the Indians, iron ore and barium sulphate on the beaches. Vancouver handed the details of his navigation over to Baker, to be worked into the chart. Then he ordered the ships made ready to sail on into Admiralty Inlet, the main passage beyond Foulweather Bluff.

# 10. Enchanted Land

IF YOU sail the inland waterways of the northwest coast of America today as a stranger, you will do so with care. The chart will be constantly open before you; lights and bell-buoys and known landmarks sign the channels from Puget Sound to Alaska and you will pay close attention to them all—or risk losing your way in the maze of twisting, rocky passages.

Vancouver had no chart, no guide, no mark of any man before him to tell him where he was or show him where to go. Only one frail thread could guide him through the maze—the jagged, unpredictable line of the continental shore, which could and did swing and turn and wander through every point of the compass. To achieve his purpose he dared never lose it, in storm or fog or snow, by night or by day, through weariness or carelessness or timidity. His boats could never pass by or turn back from even the tiniest entrance in case it might lead to the hidden passage, to some other inland sea or to a useful waterway back into the heart of the continent. He knew he must not only be faithful in this himself, but must train and trust his officers to be equally faithful.

The ships moved up, past Port Townshend and into Admiralty Inlet on a fresh breeze in brilliant weather. At the mouth of the inlet *Chatham* was sent northward to examine Rosario Strait and the Gulf Islands, while *Discovery* rode down on the breeze between the green slopes of the forest that climbed to the snow of the Olympics in the west and the snows of Mt. Baker, Mt. Rainier and the Cascade range in the east. It was a glorious world of blue and green and white—white of sail and snow and cloud, green of forest and meadow, blue of sea and sky. Menzies studied the bursting green of the maples and alders and shrubs and marvelled at the forwardness of all growth in the mild climate. Vancouver looked at the land and imagined villages, church spires, cottages and mansions scattered about the green hills. Only this was needed, he said, to make it the loveliest land on earth.

Two days after passing Port Townshend, *Discovery* anchored in the lee of a small island just south of where the city of Seattle now stands. From there Peter Puget, 2nd Lieutenant of the *Discovery*, was sent to explore the rest of the inlet; Menzies went with him in the launch and Whidbey was commanding the cutter, with both boats provisioned for a week's journey.

Puget was a man of twenty-seven or twenty-eight at this time and had already served fourteen years in the navy. Vancouver had known him before as a midshipman, during service under Sir Alan Gardner in the West Indies, and had complete faith in his skill as a surveyor.

Puget needed all his skill to unravel the tangled coast-

line of the body of water that bears his name, but he was tested in other ways too. The boats followed the shore-line southward through the narrow passage to the west of Vashon Island, held on past the future site of the city of Tacoma and by mid-afternoon rounded the point towards the big, wide bay that is now called Carr Inlet. Here they noticed two canoes full of Indians. Thus far all the Indians they had met since entering the Strait had behaved in a friendly and open way, but these dodged back and forth and kept to a wary distance in a way that made Puget uneasy. When the canoes cut across to a little cove nearby, Puget decided to follow them with the boats. The canoes were beached in front of a village and the white men could see the women and children hurrying off into the bush. As the boats came near, the canoes put off again and met them. Puget gave the Indians a few small presents and the boats landed at the village, where the men were able to trade for fresh clams. Puget even persuaded the Indians to bring some of the women and children back from the woods so that he could give them presents, too. But when the boats left the village they were still followed, at a distance, by two canoes of armed warriors. When they put into shore for the night the Indians stood off and watched as the tents were pitched, then crossed to the other side of the inlet and made their own camp.

During the night Puget took no precautions beyond the usual posting of armed sentries, but he was by no means easy about the suspicious behaviour of the Indians. He had no great experience with Indians, but he knew they were not always peaceful and harmless. Five years earlier a whole boat's crew of Captain Barkley's *Imperial Eagle* had been killed at Neah Bay, just inside the Strait of Juan de Fuca. Twelve years before that, a boat's crew of Quadra's *Sonora* had been wiped out at the same place and the little *Sonora* herself had been attacked by a war-party of over three hundred men. He remembered, too, the impaled heads and charred bones found by the boats in Port Townshend. His orders were to establish friendly relations with all the native people he met and to avoid bloodshed at all costs. But it was his duty as well to carry out his survey and protect his own people. The greatest danger, he knew, was misunderstanding, which could arise all too easily through difficulty of language. He had to be cautious and patient, yet completely firm when firmness was called for, because the natives nearly always had overwhelming superiority of numbers in a fight to the death.

But all these things were simply a part of the normal risks of exploration, and no one paid undue attention to them. They struck camp at the usual time next morning, made breakfast, loaded the boats and put off to explore Carr Inlet. As soon as they left, the Indians came across and hurried ashore to examine the camp-site. The boats continued about their business of exploration. Menzies recognized mountain ash and American ash for the first time on that side of the continent and saw pigeon guillemots nesting in cliff burrows. At one point they saw a large number of crows nesting on an island and went ashore to shoot some for fresh meat.

There were more Indians at the head of the inlet and as the boats turned back three of them put off in a canoe and followed. Like the others, these seemed suspicious and unfriendly. When Puget held up presents to encourage them to come nearer they made threatening signs and signalled the boats to go back where they had come from. Puget was still determined to win their friendship, so he fastened some pieces of iron and copper and a few medals to a board and left it floating. The Indians picked up this and other boards that were floated to them, but still would show no sign of friendship. They talked loudly among themselves about the white men, pointing to the island where the crows had been shot and making the sound "Poo Poo" to imitate the musket reports; and they called across the inlet to other Indians, drawing their attention to the

"Poo-Poo men" and evidently telling them to come on over.

It was a windless day and very hot, so Puget decided to put ashore for lunch where a small creek flowed into the inlet. Almost as the boat touched the beach, six more canoes with about twenty Indians in them came across to join the others. It was now a tense and difficult situation and everyone recognized its dangers. On shore, the superior numbers of the Indians were a hazard, and they might be joined by more canoes at any moment. But to put off again might suggest timidity and weakness that would invite attack. Puget had been going to make a set with the seine net, but he decided against this and ordered all the muskets loaded with ball. Every man was to behave normally but be on his guard; no one was to fire without orders.

Puget then walked towards the Indians and drew a plain line in the shingle with a stick, making it clear that neither side was to cross the line. The Indians seemed to accept this, which was a common custom of their own when two parties met. But they were still suspicious and hostile. They were all armed with effective bows and full quivers of arrows; some had arrows strung in the bows, others bent down to sharpen arrows on the rocks. They talked loudly among themselves, strutting boldly near the line and making gestures of contempt and challenge.

Puget went slowly back to the boats where the seamen had the meal ready. He and Menzies and Whidbey took their food and climbed on to a little bank from which they could watch both the Indians and the boats. The seamen stayed by the boats. The officers spread their meal in the sunshine, settled themselves comfortably and began to eat. Almost immediately three canoes started stealthily towards the boats. Puget ordered them back and they obeyed.

Just then another canoe loaded with Indians came in from across the inlet. The moment her prow touched, the Indians leapt out, stringing their bows, and joined the others. Together they started along the shore, across the dividing line and towards the officers. One man jumped up the bank and faced them, an arrow ready in his bow. The three officers were on their feet in an instant, muskets ready, and the seamen by the boats seized their own weapons and stood ready to fight. Puget went up to the man who had climbed the bank, thrust his musket forward at his chest and fiercely ordered the whole group back. There was a moment of hesitation, then the Indians withdrew, very slowly and reluctantly. Just across the line they stopped again and went into earnest consultation, some of them still sharpening their arrows on the rocks. Puget ordered a swivel gun to be fired from one of the boats. The Indians showed no fear of the loud explosion and the heavy splash of the shot far out on the water, but they seemed to realize that the white men were no easy mark. After another consultation they moved up to the line again, but this time they were holding out their bows and arrows, offering to trade them in the surest sign of peace and friendship.

This wise and patient behaviour of Puget and his men had its effect. The survey of the complicated waters at the head of Puget Sound took six more days and though they met Indians everywhere they went, they found nothing but friendship. It was clear that word had gone ahead that the white men in the strange craft were not afraid to fight, but could be trusted to hurt no one.

While Puget was at work in the south, the *Chatham* had

examined the islands in the northern part of the Sound and joined *Discovery* at her anchorage. As soon as Puget got back *Chatham* sailed off northward again to start Mr. Whidbey on the survey of the long narrow island that bears his name. A few days later *Discovery* followed and on June 4th the two ships were anchored in Possession Sound, near the present city of Everett. Since it was the King's birthday, Vancouver declared a holiday for all hands, with a double allowance of grog, and the best dinner the ships' supplies could offer. During the day he went ashore and took formal possession of all the land and islands northward from Cape Mendocino, on the California coast, in the name of King George III. The flag was raised, the guns fired a royal salute and Vancouver named the "interior sea" he was exploring the Gulf of Georgia.

It was over a month since they had entered the Strait of Juan de Fuca and Vancouver knew now that the work he had been sent to do would take several summers of slow, tedious and often dangerous work. He sailed from Possession Sound on the first favourable wind and took his ships round Whidbey Island to anchor in Birch Bay, a few miles south of what is now the international boundary. From there Whidbey was sent southward to explore the coastline back to Possession Sound again. Vancouver himself in the yawl, with Peter Puget in the launch, went northward into waters that would one day be Canadian.

# 11. The First Inlets

EVERY time the small boats went out from the ships they went out into the unknown. Others might have passed before them through some of the main channels, but not into the arms and inlets and not, so far as they knew, at all deeply into this inland sea. The Indians Puget had met with in the southern part of the Sound had not seen white people before, and even on Whidbey Island the chiefs had exclaimed in astonishment at Whidbey's white skin, suggesting at first that it must be painted. Vancouver remembered that Gray claimed to have gone not more than fifty miles into the strait from the ocean; it seemed unlikely that anyone else had gone farther.

This was an exciting and satisfying thought as he started northward. There might or might not be some other way out of the tangled maze of the inland sea, there might or might not be a northwest passage hidden somewhere in the broken, snow-capped immensity of the mountains; but it was quite certain there were new discoveries to be made, new peoples to be found, a coast-line utterly unknown to the civilized world to be measured and charted for the guidance of those who would come later.

Working out of Birch Bay into the wide opening of the gulf, Vancouver remembered Captain Henry Roberts, who was to have commanded the expediton, and named Point Roberts for him. From the point he looked north-westward over blue water as far as the eye could reach. Due north there was flat land and beyond that mountain ranges with deep valleys between them that promised salt water channels and inlets.

Immediately past Point Roberts the boats were able to hold well in towards shore for a little way. But they soon found themselves forced farther and farther away from the low-lying shore-line by wide and treacherous sand flats with no more than a few feet of water over them. At first Vancouver hoped to find a way over or around that would let him close in with the land again, but as the day wore on and they worked forward against the westerly breeze of the afternoon the flats became wider and shallower, often with sand-bars showing dry and stumps and driftwood piled on them. He still tried to close in with the land, but by nine o'clock at night he was seven or eight miles from it, in water that varied from one to ten fathoms. Several miles ahead was a low bluff point, but there seemed no hope of reaching land anywhere short of it, so he turned over towards the westerly side of the gulf to find a place to camp for the night. Towards one o'clock the following morning they reached a rocky place on the shore of Valdes Island where there was just room to land and cook some food. But they were forced to sleep as best they could in the open boats.

At five the next morning, after only four hours' rest, they started back across the gulf to the low bluff point which Vancouver named Point Grey. They landed there at noon to make lunch and Vancouver stood for a long while on a high place looking back towards Point Roberts. The wide shoals were plainly outlined, stretching right up to Point Grey and reaching out everywhere five miles or more from the low swampy land behind. In all the length of it, he decided, there were only two openings, both of them so narrow and shallow they could be used only by canoes. For the second time in his voyage Vancouver was making a serious error. Standing there on Point Grey, he was looking out across the mouth of the great river that would be discovered fourteen years later by Simon Fraser.

Vancouver has been much criticized for his failure to recognize the two great rivers of the Pacific northwest, but it is not really hard to understand why he failed. He was, above all things, a deep-sea sailor and not at all used to recognizing the signs of great rivers. Both the Columbia and the Fraser are glacial rivers, which bring down great quantities of silt. So the very signs by which they might have been recognized—the breakers on the Columbia River bar, and the long sand flats of the Fraser—were to Vancouver's seafaring eye extreme danger signals from which he would always be inclined to turn back. Besides this, he was looking for clear channels, something that would be of value to men with deep-sea ships, and neither river has an easy entrance.

When Vancouver looked back across the mouth of the Fraser he was already planning exploration of the long inlet he judged must lie inside Point Grey, along the line of steep mountains he could see to the northward. That same afternoon, on a pleasant westerly breeze, he sailed the small boats in through the narrow entrance to Burrard Inlet. Just through the Narrows they were met by the Capilano Indians, who put off in canoes from the north shore to greet them and offer freshly caught smelts. Vancouver was so impressed by their friendliness and courtesy that he at once ordered the boats to shorten sail and allow the canoes to keep pace. With this escort of native friends he passed by the site of the great Pacific Coast city that now bears his name. It would be nice to be able to say that he recognized the fine harbour and the other qualities that have made the city, as he had visualized the settlement that would one day come to Puget Sound. But the truth is he did not, because he had no way of knowing of the Fraser River or the railroads that would find their way down its valley or of the international boundary that would follow the 49th parallel, just north of where his ships were lying in Birch Bay.

But he was in high spirits that day and full of the delight of discovery as his boats worked up the narrow inlet. By evening they were only a mile from the head, with two or three Indian canoes still following. Once again there was only a rocky shore-line, and no good place to camp. But they landed to cook a meal and their Indian friends watched with interest as the seamen made a set with the seine net. When the net came in empty they promised to bring plenty of fish the next day. Everything about the white men fascinated them and Vancouver thoroughly enjoyed their simple curiosity, as well as their polite, considerate behaviour. All through the day they had done their best to imitate whatever they saw the white men doing and they were especially curious about the firearms.

So Vancouver loaded a musket and offered them a chance to fire it just before they left for the night. Only one of them came forward and it was a long while before he could summon up his courage to pull the trigger. But he finally did, scaring himself thoroughly and winning the admiration of all his companions.

The rocky shore-line meant another night in the boats, but two or three of the midshipmen decided that even the rocks were better than such cramped and crowded quarters, so they took their blankets ashore. They were tired boys and slept very soundly indeed. When the tide came up in the middle of the night they were half afloat before they woke up, and the disturbance ashore gave the people in the boats one final laugh in a lighthearted day.

By four o'clock the next morning they were away again, passing out of the inlet before their Indian friends were awake. The weather was dark now, with clouds scudding on a southerly breeze that freshened to a gale as they swept past Point Atkinson and into Howe Sound. And the country changed almost as the weather did. In place of the gently sloping shore-lines, the tall timber and the open meadows of Puget Sound, there were mountains on both sides that climbed almost straight from the water's edge to snow-line. Dwarfed and scattered trees clung to the dark rocks and roaring cataracts of water poured straight down the steep slopes from the snow on the mountain tops. Vancouver and all his men felt the change at once. The sound was awe-inspiring, desolate and oppressive under the threatening clouds, like a world before life was born. Nothing moved in it except the tumbling waterfalls; they could imagine no life existing there. Yet, as the gale carried them forward and the mountains closed in behind them, Vancouver sat forward at the tiller of the yawl with an excitement he could hardly conceal. They were passing between the mountains, deeper and deeper into them. Perhaps this was the passage that would lead through and beyond them.

Through the afternoon the hope held. Then they came within sight of the swampy ground at the head of the inlet and saw the mountains massed beyond it, higher, more formidable and more rugged than any they had passed. Wearily they turned back, expecting to spend another night in the boats along the inhospitable shore-line. Then, just before dark, they found a little cove with a stretch of level land and hurried ashore to pitch the tents for the first time since leaving the ships. It was barely done before a fierce wind struck from the south, bringing torrents of rain that drove upon them in squalls all through the night and kept them ashore until late the following morning.

As soon as the storm let up the boats put off again and during the next three or four days they worked up the Gulf of Georgia, inside Texada Island and into the fifty-mile length of Jervis Inlet. Here again hopes built high as they passed deeper and deeper into the mountains and the inlet held its width. Vancouver remembered the inland sea of the old pilot Juan de Fuca, a hundred or a hundred and twenty miles broad; the claims of de Fonte and all the other old tales that might bear some shade or hint of long lost truth. But the inlet ended at last, as the others had, in low swampy land and a deep valley leading still farther back among the mountains.

The boats were now six days away from the ships with only a week's supply of food, but Vancouver chose deliberately to follow the longer, unexplored way out of the inlet to the north of Nelson Island, hoping it would lead to some point farther up the Gulf to which he could then take his ships. The men, he believed, would have learned by experience that the boat trips seldom ended when they were supposed to and would have kept back some of their supplies to take care of this. He must have been right, because it was altogether eleven days before they got back to the ships again. But on the way they had at least one unexpected meal.

Rowing southward towards Point Grey early in the morning of Friday, June 22nd, they saw two ships at anchor. At first Vancouver thought Broughton had moved *Discovery* and *Chatham* forward without orders. As the boats drew nearer he could see that these were small ships, flying the Spanish flag, the *Sutil* and *Mexicana*.

It was an unpleasant shock to find them here, in waters he believed his were the first ships, certainly the first naval ships, to enter. Hungry and exhausted as he was, and as he knew his crews must be, Vancouver felt resentment and even hostility. But this was a personal feeling that he thrust firmly aside as the boats came up to the Spanish ships. He stepped aboard as a naval officer and the King's Commissioner, saluting the Spanish flag, meeting the courtesy and grace of the Spanish captains, Galiano and Valdes, with a matching courtesy and the pride and dignity of his rank and service.

They were all men and all seamen, and the Spanish captains were immediately concerned with the state of Vancouver and his people after their long spell in the open boats. A fine meal was soon ready for them all and the Spaniards offered to send a boat of their own to guide Vancouver's ships forward to Point Grey while he and his men rested aboard. Vancouver declined the offer, saying he was anxious to get back aboard *Discovery* and continue his survey. But he sat at breakfast with them in Galiano's tiny cabin aboard the *Sutil*, and soon the three captains were talking freely of the things that touched them most closely.

The *Sutil* and the *Mexicana*, Vancouver learned, were part of the command of Señor Malaspina, detached to continue exploration of the Gulf of Georgia, started by other Spanish ships the previous year. They knew the Gulf northward as far as the north of Texada Island which was, as Vancouver had supposed it might be, an island and not a peninsula. But they had kept to the open waters and knew nothing of Puget Sound or any of the long inlets.

They spoke also of the Rio Blanca which they, like Vancouver, had been unable to find, though it was shown on the old Spanish maps. And they said that Señor Quadra, the commander-in-chief of the Spanish Navy in Mexico, was already at Nootka, waiting for Vancouver's arrival to hand over the lands assigned to Great Britain in the Nootka Convention.

As he talked with the Spanish captains, Vancouver studied their ships. They were, he decided, quite unfitted for the difficult work they had to do. Neither was larger than forty-five tons, with only two brass guns and the most cramped and uncomfortable quarters for the twenty-four men and one officer who served in each of them. They were well supplied with good food and wine, but there was little else to suggest that the great Spanish nation was taking proper care of the brave men who carried its flag into the far places of the sea. Vancouver already liked the two young Spanish captains, and gladly agreed to their suggestion that the two expeditions might well join forces to explore the Gulf of Georgia and whatever lay beyond it.

Through the rest of that day, against two flood tides, the boats' crews rowed back across the wide mouth of the still undiscovered river. They camped for the night at Point Roberts and reached the ships in Birch Bay the following morning, after a journey of over three hundred miles.

# 12. The Way Through

JUNE 24TH, 1792, was a lovely day and Vancouver's ships joined the Spanish ships at about two in the afternoon. The crews saluted each other by cheering, Galiano and Valdes came aboard *Discovery* to spend the afternoon with Vancouver, and the four ships sailed on together up the Gulf of Georgia on a fine fresh breeze.

The breeze fell away at sunset and did not freshen again till the following afternoon, when the ships passed the northern end of Texada Island and found anchorage after dark in Desolation Sound. Through much of the journey the Spanish captains had been with Vancouver, exchanging information, studying charts and trying to guess at where the inland sea would lead them. Was there or was there not a way through it to the north? Galiano and Valdes told Vancouver they had talked often with Gray and were quite sure he had never made any such voyage as that shown on Meare's map. Valdes, who spoke the Indian languages quite fluently, said that natives had told him there was a way through to the ocean in the north, but added that he knew them too well to put much faith in what they said. Vancouver had expected that the Spaniards would have much more exact information than he about the discoveries of de Fonte and de Fuca, and he was more amused than disappointed to find that they were expecting exactly the same thing of him. When they had talked themselves out and examined every chart and rumour, it was completely clear that they were in new waters; no white man before them had been beyond the north end of Texada Island and no one could know what lay ahead of them.

At daylight on the morning of Tuesday the 26th, Vancouver came on deck to study the land ahead of *Discovery*'s uncomfortable anchorage in Desolation Sound. It was not an encouraging prospect. The Sound itself was steep-walled and rocky. It was clear that with the two pleasant islands he had named just north of Texada, Harwood and Savary, they had come to the end of the broad and easy waters of the gulf. Everywhere ahead, to north and west, the mountains were massed against them, rising straight up from the water in range upon range. Hidden somewhere amongst them was the twisting line of the continental shore. It was time for the small boats to go out again.

Vancouver sent Puget and Whidbey south to trace the shore-line backward to the last point they had recognized from the ships. Johnstone was to work northward, while Galiano and Valdes offered to explore whatever lay eastward, between the other two parties. So it happened that Johnstone, the quiet, efficient master of the *Chatham*, made one of the greatest discoveries of the whole voyage.

The first stage of Johnstone's exploration took him up

the long monotonous reach of Bute Inlet, between high grey-green mountains to the double valley at the head. From there he turned back along the opposite shore. Nearing the entrance of the inlet again, he came upon a settlement of friendly Indians who eagerly traded herrings and other fish for nails. Just beyond the settlement was a narrow passage that seemed to lead out of the inlet. Johnstone took his boat into it against a strong tide that increased as the passage narrowed. Soon it was too much for the men at the oars and the boat was swept back. The Indians saw them in trouble and at once came down to help, clambering over the rocky shores to pull and heave on the ropes and gunwales with the seamen. In the end the boat got through to a wider channel where the tides were still strong and confused.

Studying it, Johnstone realized that the flood tide was running southward, out of the passage, exactly against the direction of the tides they had seen so far. He thought of going on, but supplies were already low and he knew there was no chance of completing the exploration. It was raining heavily, with a thick haze over the water and the second boat, under young Spelman Swaine, had not yet come through the rapids, so he turned back.

While Johnstone was away the other boats had explored the many passages and islands near Desolation Sound. Zachary Mudge, the *Discovery*'s first lieutenant, had landed on one of the islands with Mr. Menzies and climbed to the top of a high mountain. From it they had seen a high bluff point with what seemed to be a wide inlet behind it, at some distance away to the west. As soon as they reported this, Vancouver sent them to examine it. Johnstone reached the ships on July 2nd and left again with a week's provisions the next day. Three days later Mudge and Menzies came back with news that the channel beyond Cape Mudge was wide and deep, with no apparent ending in the ten or twelve miles they had travelled into it. Here again the tides were strong and regular, and the flood came down from the northwestward. Gradually the confused pattern of the inland waterways was becoming clearer. It was certain now that they were far from the end of them and that there might well be a way through to the ocean again.

Vancouver could only wait impatiently for Johnstone's return. Desolation Sound was a poor anchorage. It offered little in the way of fresh supplies and little chance for work or recreation of any kind ashore. The overshadowing mountains and rocky, precipitous shores were depressing to officers and men alike. Only the pleasant companionship of the Spanish ships and the ready friendship of their crews relieved the monotony. A week passed and Johnstone still had not returned. Impatience became anxiety, as it would again and again while Vancouver awaited the return of his little boats from their expeditions. The possibilities of accident or injury were all too many—fierce tides, stormy seas, hostile Indians and unknown dangers beyond these in the unknown country. The problems of search and rescue could be enormous, even fatal to the success of the expedition. Vancouver was well aware of all these dangers and he always worried and fretted when his little boats were late. The crews that manned them were his people; it was his duty to risk them, but it was equally his duty to bring them safely home.

Johnstone and Spelman Swaine had gone straight into unknown danger. They passed the main entrance to Bute

Inlet and at once came into the treacherous, broken length of the Yuculta Rapids. The fierce currents swirled and tore at the little boats, whirlpools sucked at them behind the islands, foaming overfalls rushed down to break against them, great boils of water surged up to toss them within feet of the rocky shores. Through all this the leadsman took soundings and Johnstone and Swaine studied the islands and the twists of the channel, trying to judge whether there could be some way of bringing the big ships safely through.

In time the channel widened and the strength of the tide eased a little. But now the continental shore-line was broken again. Towards nightfall they reached the mouth of Loughborough Inlet and camped on a rocky island. During the night the flood tide came down from north-westward, four hours earlier than the tides of the Gulf of Georgia and several feet higher. It forced them to move their camp farther up the rocky slope, and when they were settled again Johnstone lay in his blankets puzzling over it all. If the flood tide came from the northwestward, then the ocean must be somewhere in that general direction. If it was four hours ahead of the gulf tides, then it matched almost exactly with the tides at Nootka. There was little doubt in his mind that he was near the northern entrance of the inland sea. But how near? His orders were to follow the continental shore-line without fail. How many long inlets must he follow out before he could find the way through?

The next day the boats traced out the forty-mile shore-line of Loughborough Inlet. Then Johnstone made his decision. He forgot about the continental shore-line, worked north through the rough tides of Wellbore Channel and rounded the northern side of Hardwicke Island into the wide, straight channel that is now Johnstone's Strait.

Their way up the strait was made slow and difficult by strong westerly winds that blew against them during the days and the thick mists that came down at night and lasted through the early mornings. But the country was more attractive now, with islands of moderate height to the eastward and a western shore-line that sloped almost gently back to high, snow-capped mountains. Indian canoes passed and re-passed everywhere along the shores. Some of the Indians had muskets and all were used to white men. Johnstone stopped briefly to visit Cheslakees village at the mouth of the Nimpkish River, then pressed on again because his supplies were already low.

A short distance beyond Cheslakees the strait became very wide, with small islands dotted all across it. They had an east wind now, with heavy rain, and Johnstone held on until dark in the hope of getting sight of the ocean. At dusk the weather was so bad that they had to anchor in the lee of a small island. All through that night, through the next day and the following night, the wind blew and the rain poured down while they huddled wretchedly in the anchored boats. But the morning of July 10th was clear, with a westerly breeze. Johnstone picked out a small island, rowed over to it and went ashore. From the height of the island they could see the wide unbroken expanse of the ocean. They had found the way through.

They were six days and over a hundred and twenty miles from the ships now, with provisions running very short. Johnstone wasted no time in celebration. The westerly wind was with them and both boats set sail and rode through until midnight, when they camped on the shore of Hardwicke Island. From there Johnstone hoped to follow the new channel down until it came out, as he felt sure it would, into the arm that Mudge and Menzies had seen from the mountain top. At first the channel led on, as he had hoped it would, towards the southwest, a clear, easy passage nearly two miles wide and without dangerous tides. Then it swung almost due southward.

Once again Johnstone made a hard decision. His men had been rationed to one small meal a day for the past two days and now they had nothing left. If the southward channel should lead too far from the ships or end against another blank wall of mountains, they would be facing starvation. From Chatham Point he turned into Nodales Channel, rode the Yuculta Rapids again and reached the ships in Desolation Sound at 2 a.m. on July 12th, after nine days of exhausting and difficult work.

As soon as he had Johnstone's report, Vancouver was sure that the channel beyond Cape Mudge would lead him through to Johnstone Strait and so to the open sea. Johnstone's observations of latitude and longitude, sketched on to the charts, made it even more certain. He shared all the new information with Galiano and Valdes and asked them to come on with him, but they felt their slow ships would delay *Discovery* and *Chatham*. They said they preferred to explore Johnstone's route for themselves, in their own time and would meet Vancouver again at Nootka.

Vancouver sailed from Desolation Sound in high spirits. It felt fine to be out of the place, with the long open sweep of the Gulf in sight again and whales playing about the ships as they sailed among the pleasant islands towards Cape Mudge. Early in the afternoon they rounded the Cape and anchored just off the Indian village, half a mile inside it. There, for the first time, Vancouver saw for himself the flood tide setting southward. There was no longer doubt in his mind that this was the way he must go, since Johnstone had reported the Yucultas all but impossible for a ship as large as the *Discovery*. But he sent Puget and Whidbey out in the small boats to scout the passage through to where Johnstone had left it, and two more boats to find another anchorage for the ships farther up the inlet.

During the afternoon Vancouver and Menzies went ashore to return the visit of the Indians who had come out to the ships as they anchored. More than seventy canoes, some of them quite large, were drawn up on the beach at the foot of the bluff where they landed, and the chief welcomed them there, then led them up a steep, narrow path to the village itself. There were twelve great houses, planked with cedar boards and decorated with bright paintings. The people sat in front of them, waiting to talk with the visitors. The two white men walked slowly along, handing out such presents as they had with them and enjoyed the obvious friendship of the quiet, orderly people. Later they walked for about two miles northward along the flat land above the water, with several of the Indians following and picking berries, which they passed to Vancouver or Menzies on broad green thimbleberry leaves.

The next day the ships moved forward about twelve miles to a safe anchorage in Nymphe Cove, on the north side of the big bay just south of Seymour Narrows. Menzies, as usual, went ashore to look for plants, but found nothing new except a pentstemon. It was, he remarked, a rocky, hilly, barren sort of place. But today the big bay is called Menzies Bay and the massive mountain behind it is Menzies Mountain.

Vancouver watched the fierce tides of Seymour Narrows from the shelter of the bay, noticing their tremendous force and the wild turbulence that broke into foaming white waves like waterfalls. But he believed there was nothing more than the force of the water, no rock or obstruction to cause the turbulence. And when Puget and Whidbey came back with the news that there was no other difficulty between Nymphe Cove and Johnstone Strait except these narrows, he took his ships through on the first ebb-tide. He saw nothing of the great rock that rears up in mid-channel, barely nine feet under at low water, though both ships drew water enough to strike it if they had been unlucky.

Early on Monday, July 16, the ships rounded Chatham Point into Johnstone Strait. It seemed now that all the hazards of the inland sea were safely passed and the way to the ocean lay clear ahead.

# 13. Perilous Passage

THE real story of George Vancouver is not in one great voyage or in any one spectacular deed. It is in the hundreds of lesser voyages made by the small boats, in the persistence and thoroughness and unfailing courage with which these were carried out through three long years of exploration. Many people share in the story—Broughton and Puget and Mudge, Johnstone, Whidbey, Swaine, as well as the seamen who rowed the boats and endured the constant hardships and risks of the survey. Vancouver was the driving force behind them, his was the strength that held them all together, the wisdom and judgment and devotion that brought them safely through, a community of men in two small ships ten thousand miles away from their nearest base of supply.

Now that the mystery of the inside passage was solved, a less dedicated man might have chosen to head out for the open sea and down to Nootka. There was important work to be done there and Quadra had already been waiting for several months. But Vancouver read over his orders again, as he had many times before, and decided that they called for him to be in two places at once—at Nootka, as the King's Commissioner, and out along the coast-line searching for the northwest passage. He had searched the coast through little more than four degrees of latitude in the better part of a season; he still had to search nine degrees farther north under conditions that would grow constantly more difficult. The remaining six weeks of summer weather were far too valuable to lose and he knew he must use them to carry his survey as far northward as possible.

As soon as the ships rounded Chatham Point into Johnstone Strait the small boats went out again, to pick up the continental shore-line where Johnstone had left it in Wellbore Channel. The work went well. Broughton took the little *Chatham* safely through the rock-broken tides of Chatham Channel, where coastal steamers still strike all too often, and sailed her up the eighty-mile reach of Knight Inlet and back again, then northward to Deepsea Bluff. From there Vancouver himself took the yawl through Kingcome Inlet, McKenzie Sound and Drury Inlet, then out by Wells Pass to Queen Charlotte Strait.

The shore-line ahead now seemed straight and compact along the northern side of the wide strait, leading towards small, scattered islands in the distance, so it was time to bring the ships forward again and find a passage for them. At first it was plain sailing, in spite of fog and light winds. But by the morning of August 6th they had reached the scattered islands and found themselves among rocks as well as islands, some showing above water, some just awash, some completely hidden by the easy lap of the waves. The breeze died and the fog came down again, hiding everything. For several hours the ships drifted helplessly, with no bottom the anchors could reach.

It was a breathless, agonizing time in which there was nothing to do but wait and pray and peer out into the clinging, silent whiteness that swirled over the smooth grey surface of the sea. Men stood by their posts in the silence, feeling the drip of moisture from masts and rigging, listening for the lap of water against rock, waiting for the grinding jar that might signal the end of *Chatham* or *Discovery* or of both ships. Then, towards noon, a little, light breeze from the northwest lifted the fog and broke it into wisps and wraiths that slowly spread away to southward. The ships were squarely in the centre of the channel Vancouver had chosen between the islands. But the rocks were still all about them, ahead and astern, scattered away to the southward for as far as the eye could reach. Vancouver had two choices. He could steer among them in search of an anchorage, then send the boats out to find a better passage; or he could try to sail through, trusting to a sharp look-out and quick handling of the ships. He chose to sail.

For three or four hours all went well as the ships twisted and dodged among the rocks. Then, at about 4 p.m., the *Discovery* struck and was held fast on a falling tide. *Chatham* anchored in fifty fathoms a short distance away and at once sent all her boats.

It was a desperate situation. The force with which the ship had struck had raised her bow several feet out of the water and the ebbing tide left her still farther out forward and deeper astern. Vancouver worked methodically, but swiftly. First the stream anchor was carried out astern. The men heaved on it with the capstan, trying to wrench the

ship free, but only tore the anchor from its holding. As soon as this failed the yards and top-masts were struck and used to shore up the ship on the starboard side, to which she was beginning to list heavily. Then the work of lightening ship began. Fresh water was emptied from the casks, fuel and ballast were thrown overboard, as much as possible of the heavier supplies were loaded into the small boats. A sudden freak of the tide swung the ship's stern, so that she heeled still more dangerously. The men worked feverishly to force new props in place, but she was far over, the bulwarks amidships within three inches of the water.

All this while the sea was dead calm. Vancouver knew, and every man with him knew, that the least swell starting in from the open sea would mean loss of the ship. At nine o'clock, still in daylight, still in dead calm, the ebb-tide reached its lowest point. Vancouver left nothing to chance. With the bow in three feet of water and the stern over four fathoms, the work of lightening ship went on. Soon after midnight the props began to fall free as the ship lifted to the incoming tide. By two in the morning she was nearly upright. One easy heave on the anchor floated her, free and undamaged.

But the graveyard of rocks still stretched ahead between the ships and the open sea. Vancouver gave his men three hours' rest, then the work of re-stowing the ship began. By noon she was ready to sail again. An hour later, on a light breeze from the southwest, the ships moved on.

There was a surf now, breaking everywhere on rocky islets and hidden rocks. But they were bound to go on, trusting seamanship and ready crews to take them out of that fearful place in weather that was still moderate. By five o'clock in the afternoon the channel was wider and the worst seemed to be over. Then the wind fell away to intermittent breezes that died almost as the sails filled, stole up from some other direction and died away again. Once more the ships were drifting helplessly on the ebb-tide, and at six o'clock the *Chatham* struck a ledge of hidden rocks. The *Discovery* was about three miles away at the time, but she dropped anchor immediately and sent away the small boats. The exhausted officers and men faced another night of struggle to save the ship, and this time the danger seemed greater than before as the swell was heavy enough to make her lift and pound on the rocks at each surge. But Broughton sent word back to Vancouver that she had struck lightly and was pounding lightly; he expected no serious damage unless the swells increased, and as the tide was already half ebbed when she struck she would certainly float with the flood.

Even so, it was necessary to lighten the ship and prop her with every available spar and yard. All they had were not enough and as the tide ebbed she hung precariously threatening to heel over beyond possibility of righting. Then a chance of the tide brought down a length of driftwood that was exactly what they needed. The men seized it eagerly and forced it into place. Soon after midnight, on the returning tide, the *Chatham* floated free.

It was two more days before the ships finally worked their way out of the rock-strewn strait into open water. Vancouver worked northward to Safety Cove in Fitzhugh Sound, recognizing the waters he was now in from the charts of Captain James Hanna, one of the earliest of the fur-traders. The small boats went out again to explore the nearby arms and inlets, working in cold, wet weather which warned that the end of the summer was near. Then, on August 18th, the brig *Venus*, an Indian fur-trader, came in from Nootka. Her captain had a letter for Vancouver from the supply ship *Daedalus* at Nootka. The commander of the *Daedalus*, Mr. Richard Hergest, with Mr. Gooch, an astronomer on his way out to join the expedition, and a seaman, had been killed by natives in the Hawaiian Islands.

Deeply disturbed by this news and concerned for the health of his men in the increasingly cold weather, Vancouver decided to end the season's work and go back to Nootka.

# 14. Señor Don Quadra

VANCOUVER supposed, as he sailed towards Nootka, that his duty there would be a simple formality. His orders, he felt, were perfectly clear. He would receive from Señor Quadra, Representative of His Catholic Majesty, the King of Spain, surrender of all land and property seized from John Meares, both at Nootka and at Port Cox, a few miles to the south. And both sides would formally recognize the other terms of the Nootka Convention, especially the provision that the whole coast of America north from San Francisco would from then on be open for trade and settlement to British and Spanish on equal terms. Vancouver knew that these were weighty concessions, amounting to retreat, from the proud claims Spain had always made in the Pacific Ocean. But the terms had been agreed upon in London and Madrid. They matched with his own idea of the failing power of Spain and the growing strength of Britain. He expected no difficulty.

Señor Don Juan Francisco de la Bodega y Quadra was a

Spaniard of the New World. Born in Lima, Peru, of a noble Spanish family, he had reached his high position as Commander-in-Chief of the Spanish naval forces at San Blas only by conspicuous ability and devoted service; it was a rare thing for anyone born outside Spain to be given an important appointment in the Spanish possessions.

Quadra had first proved himself a superb seaman when he took the schooner, *Sonora*, northward from Mexico as far as the coast of Alaska in 1775. He was about thirty years old then, and must have been brave as a lion, for he took his tiny ship much farther than his commander, Don Bruno Hecata dared to go in his far larger *Santiago*. Four years later Quadra commanded an expedition of his own which followed the coast-line to 61°N. and did much valuable work for Spain. Since that time he had risen steadily to his present position of command. He was not the sort of Spaniard to yield anything more than he had to. He had come to Nootka prepared to yield nothing at all.

*Discovery* and *Chatham* sailed into Friendly Cove at Nootka on 28th August, 1792. Vancouver saluted the Spanish flag with thirteen guns and the salute was immediately returned by the brig *Activa*, at anchor in the harbour and flying Quadra's pennant. Quadra himself was ashore, but at once sent a courteous request that Vancouver and his officers visit him that evening.

They went ashore in their best uniforms, with everything brushed and polished and cleaned till it shone. A guard of honour was drawn up on the beach and Quadra and his officers met the visitors at the doorway of his residence, a substantial two-storey building with a balcony and other touches of Spanish architecture. It was a formal greeting, yet a warm and friendly one, and the

Spanish officers led their British guests upstairs to the great hall of the residence. Quadra asked at once for details of the voyage and Vancouver gave them to him through Mr. Dobson, one of the mates of the *Daedalus,* who spoke fluent Spanish. Before they left, Quadra offered every hospitality of the port, his ship and his residence, and promised to bring his officers to breakfast aboard *Discovery* next morning.

Both Quadra and Vancouver had formed an instant liking for each other, which grew with every hour they were together and spread among their officers and men. The breakfast aboard the *Discovery* soon broke down all difficulties of language and custom, and the rest of the day was a glorious holiday, ending in a magnificent dinner ashore and salutes of twenty-one guns to the Kings of England and Spain.

It was after this that the negotiations began, with a long letter from Quadra to Vancouver, which Dobson translated. To Vancouver's surprise and concern, the letter went back over the whole history of the northwest coast, from the earliest Spanish voyages to the expedition of Martinez which had seized Meares' ships. Quadra's conclusions were that Martinez behaved quite properly in seizing the ships, that Meares had had no real title to any land at all and no buildings larger than a temporary hut; so there was, in fact, nothing to hand back. Besides all this, Quadra went on, it was quite clear that Nootka was the most northerly Spanish settlement; from there on, the coast would be open equally to British and Spanish; but southward from Nootka everything belonged to Spain.

All this was explained most politely and reasonably. And Quadra made it clear he did not want to be difficult.

It was most important for their two great nations to settle things in a friendly way that would make for lasting peace. So he would withdraw his garrison to Neah Bay, in the Strait of Juan de Fuca, leaving everything at Nootka for Vancouver's convenience, with the clear understanding that this would in no way affect the legal rights of Spain in the port.

Quadra was sincere in all this. He had known the northwest coast intimately for twenty years. He was the man on the spot, and he could not believe that rights he had accepted since childhood had been signed away in a treaty made on the other side of the world.

Vancouver met him just as sincerely and just as firmly. He could not, he explained, go over the past history of the affair; that had already been argued out between the Ministers of State, who had also decided the terms of the treaty. He was there to receive back Port Nootka and Port Cox, and his orders gave him no power to settle for anything less. He was bound to consider any Spanish settlement north of San Francisco, including the one at Neah Bay, a "port of free access", open to British and Spanish alike. But he had no wish to shorten Quadra's time in Nootka and would be happy to have him stay ashore until the alterations to the *Activa* were finished.

This exchange had taken several days, but it made absolutely no difference to the good fellowship between the Spaniards and British, and it only increased the respect and affection Vancouver and Quadra felt for each other. On the evening of their arrival Quadra had opened the port to the British with what seemed extravagant words; the British officers, he had said, were to treat his residence as their home and the more they used it the happier he would be. Vancouver was to demand anything he needed, for his men or his ships. Now every meal was a celebration, aboard *Discovery* or *Chatham* or in the great hall of the residence. Spanish blacksmiths wrought iron for the ships, Spanish bakers baked bread and Spanish cordage went into the blocks and rigging to replace worn British rope. There was so much saluting back and forth, Menzies remarked, the British ships puffing away with the best of them, that there was not enough powder aboard to fight off a determined Indian attack and the ships had to borrow more from the Spanish magazines before they left the post.

But Quadra showed his generosity and good faith best of all in the help he gave Vancouver in dealing with Maquinna, the great Nootka chief. Maquinna was fond of the Spaniards and very proud of the trust they placed in him. He came out to the *Discovery* soon after she anchored, unannounced and with nothing to distinguish him from any of his subjects. To his indignation he was turned off by the sentry on watch and he went at once to tell Quadra of the indignity he had suffered. Quadra did his best to explain the misunderstanding and told Vancouver what to do about it. With a few handsome presents and a pressing invitation to breakfast aboard *Discovery* next morning, Maquinna's injured dignity seemed much restored.

But at breakfast, after a few glasses of wine, the matter came up again. Maquinna said he was sorry the Spaniards were leaving. He didn't like the British, they didn't know how to treat him and even if they learned they would probably leave and hand him over to some other country. It was a perfect opportunity for Quadra to make trouble and ill feeling had he chosen to. Instead, he told Maquinna that the British were fine people, that they would treat him and his people every bit as kindly and courteously as the Spaniards had and he could trust them completely. To Vancouver's surprise Maquinna listened closely and seemed to accept what Quadra said in perfect faith. It was clear from this and from the excellent behaviour of the Indians at all times that they held the Spaniards in very high esteem.

But Quadra did not leave the matter there. A few days later he suggested to Vancouver a ceremonial visit to Maquinna, who had moved to his royal residence at the head of Tahsis Inlet. It was perfect weather, so they started out the next morning; Vancouver, Quadra and several Spanish officers travelled together in the *Discovery*'s yawl, and as many Spanish and British officers as could crowd in followed in three other small boats.

It was a warm, sunny day and the boats made good progress up the long, narrow inlet between the towering mountains. An escort of Indian canoes soon joined them and the boats made a brave show for them, with drums and fifes playing lively military tunes that carried over the smooth water and echoed bravely back from the mountains.

Maquinna welcomed them with joy. The scarlet uniforms of the marines, the trimness of the boats, the ceremonial precision of the landing-parties all stirred his pride and made him even greater in the eyes of his people. He was celebrating the coming of age of his eldest daughter, a plump, pretty, well-mannered girl of fifteen or sixteen, whom he had just declared the heiress of all his power and property. The arrival of the visitors fitted perfectly with this and made the great occasion still more splendid.

111

Quadra, as usual, had brought with him an abundance of good food and wine and the sailors prepared a great meal while the officers paid a respectful visit to the Princess in Maquinna's lodge. After that Maquinna and the Princess came back with them to the banquet, the Princess sitting at the head of the table and behaving most graciously in that company of men. When the meal was over Maquinna put on a great display of war-dances, taking part in some of them himself with tremendous energy and humour that delighted all his people. Vancouver had his seamen sing a few songs and dance some reels in return, then the party broke up with Maquinna's promise to return the visit within a few days.

As they travelled down the inlet next day, Vancouver and Quadra stopped for lunch on some sun-warmed rocks along the shore. They were still trying to agree on the terms of the treaty—there had been another exchange of letters between them just before they left Friendly Cove—but their friendship was now warm and complete and they never discussed the issue when they were to-gether. There were so many other things to discuss. Both were seamen of the highest order; both were commanders in the world's proudest navies; both knew the Pacific coast of North America as no other men in the world knew it at that time. In their brief knowledge of each other, neither had said or done anything small or underhanded; they had met as men of honour, dealt as men of honour and learned to love each other in the dealing.

As the meal ended, Quadra spoke of this. It was, he said, too fine and rare a thing to be forgotten, and he asked Vancouver to commemorate it by naming some port or island after them both. Without hesitation, Vancouver turned round and swung his arm in a great semicircle from southeast to northwest to suggest the mass of land round which he had just brought his ships. This, he said, should be the island of Quadra and Vancouver. And for many years it was, though the big island has now become Vancouver Island and a smaller, sister island between Vancouver Island and the mainland is Quadra Island.

About two weeks later Quadra sailed from Nootka for the Spanish port of Monterey. Vancouver had refused to take over Nootka on Quadra's terms and both men had agreed to refer the matter to their respective governments. On October 12th Vancouver also sailed from Nootka, with *Discovery, Chatham* and *Daedalus,* to rejoin Quadra at Monterey.

On the way south he detached the *Daedalus* to explore Gray's Harbour, then tried to enter the mouth of the Columbia River with *Discovery* and *Chatham*. After two days in the breakers, *Discovery* was forced to turn away from the river and continue her voyage southward. But the *Chatham,* which drew three feet less water, won through after being almost swamped and again losing her jolly-boat. Broughton explored the river for about forty miles from its mouth, then followed Vancouver southward.

# 15. King Tamaahmaah

THE ships had a long stay in Monterey, made possible by Quadra's broad and generous interpretation of the laws of hospitality. The pleasant round of visits and parties was taken up again and soon became as free and lively as it had been at Nootka. All the ships' crews were able to go out into the countryside on excursions and picnics. There were grand dinners and entertainments, and even dances, for many of the Spanish soldiers had their wives and families with them in the garrison.

The ships were able to take aboard ample supplies of fresh meat and vegetables, and the early signs of scurvy which had shown up in the *Discovery* on the way south quickly disappeared. It was exactly the kind of holiday that everyone needed after the hard summer's work and the long voyage before it. Yet when Vancouver offered to make the usual payment for all the provisions and other supplies, Quadra brushed the matter lightly aside. It was not, he said, worth discussing. If the Spanish and British governments thought it worth while, let them worry about it and settle accounts between them.

Vancouver and Quadra did not reopen their diplomatic discussions, but Quadra told Vancouver he had orders from Spain to seize all foreign ships that appeared along the coast except the British. From this they decided that their two governments were still working together and would send new instructions in time. Vancouver had already sent Zachary Mudge to England with despatches aboard a trading-vessel from Nootka, but the whole matter seemed so important and so difficult that he was planning to send the *Chatham* with all the charts and other information he had. Now he decided to send Broughton alone, and Quadra at once offered to take him to Mexico and get a passage for him in a ship sailing from the Atlantic coast.

Towards the middle of January the two commanders sailed from Monterey with their little fleets. In good weather and with fine fresh winds, *Discovery* and *Activa* soon outsailed the others and it was clear that the *Activa* was faster than *Discovery*. But Quadra shortened sail a little and the two sailed on together a cable's length or less apart. The two captains and their officers visited constantly back and forth from ship to ship, clinging to their cheerful companionship until the last possible moment. But Vancouver's true course was westward for the Hawaiian Islands and Quadra's southeastward for San Blas in Mexico, so all too soon it was time to separate. On the last evening they could hold together, Quadra, Broughton and all the Spanish officers who could be spared from duty came over to the *Discovery* for a farewell dinner.

It was a lovely evening, with a calm sea and light breezes

that kept the ships moving slowly and smoothly ahead under gently drawing sails that shone like snow in the moonlight. The wine passed again and again in the crowded cabin on *Discovery*'s quarter-deck. Toasts were drunk to England, to Spain, to Vancouver and Quadra and the good fellowship between their fleets, to future successes and future meetings. But at midnight it was time to separate, and there on the sparkling sea, two hundred miles due west of the present boundary between California and Mexico, the two great captains said good-bye for the last time. They had known each other for less than six months, the barrier of language stood between them and agreement upon the great affairs with which they were charged had proved impossible. Yet one of the warmest and most generous friendships in history had somehow reached across all these obstacles and become perfect. Vancouver felt they would not meet again, and his heart was heavy with a sense of loss as he swung his ship westward towards the islands.

He changed course only to head towards a new and very different friendship. The three ships reached the Hawaiian Islands towards the middle of February. *Daedalus* sailed on for Australia, to bring back supplies and new orders from England during the course of the following season. *Discovery* and *Chatham* put in towards the island of Hawaii and were met by two or three small canoes. The natives in them brought word that the whole island would be under a religious taboo for the next few days, so no other canoes were allowed to put off. When the taboo was lifted Kahowmotoo, the local chief under King Tamaahmaah, would welcome the ships. But King Tamaahmaah had placed a taboo on all trading with European ships except for firearms and ammunition, which he needed to continue his conquest of the other islands.

There was a good deal in all this for Vancouver to think about. His orders were to winter in the islands, replenish his supplies there and complete their survey. But there was much more to be done than this. Since Cook's death, things had changed greatly in the islands. They had become an important provisioning station for ships of many nations. The natives were intelligent, brave and ambitious. Several times in the past few years they had successfully attacked European ships and killed the crews, and though the Europeans had usually been at fault these successes had made the islands a very dangerous place for visiting ships. In addition, a long series of tribal wars was laying waste the land, destroying livestock and keeping the people from their work in the fields. Vancouver was determined to do his best to change all this and make the islands safe and useful again. He was also determined to find and punish the murderers of Lieutenant Hergest and William Gooch.

He remembered Tamaahmaah, from Cook's last voyage, as the fiercest-looking warrior he had ever seen in the South Seas, a huge and powerful young man who even then was an important leader. Now, after fourteen years, it seemed that Tamaahmaah was the most powerful of all the warring chiefs and was already King of Hawaii, the largest island. Vancouver had been warned that he had several brass cannons mounted on the shore of Karakakoa Bay and plenty of ammunition for them, but it was clear that Tamaahmaah and no one else was the man he must deal with.

As soon as the taboo was lifted, Kahowmotoo came off

to welcome the ships. He was an oldish man, kindly and gentle, though still very much a chief and a warrior. Vancouver met him courteously, but told him at once that the English ships would not trade in firearms—the ships and all the arms aboard them belonged to King George, and he had tabooed such trade. Kahowmotoo was disappointed, but he accepted the taboo as something both he and Vancouver were bound to respect and at once busied himself in arranging for fat hogs and fresh vegetables to be sent aboard in exchange for ordinary trade goods. Another important chief, Tianna, also came in with supplies, and as soon as these were loaded Vancouver sailed to meet the King of Karakakoa Bay, taking Kahowmotoo and Tianna with him.

Tamaahmaah came out to the ships when they were still at some distance from the bay, and he met them in friendship and high good humour, bringing his favourite wife, Tahowmannoo, aboard with him. Studying the King, Vancouver saw at once that he was a different man from the fierce young chief he had known before. He was still an immensely powerful man, every inch a warrior and full of vigour. But he, like Vancouver's other friend Pomurrey, had grown into a calm, wise man, cheerful and good-humoured, but with all the natural dignity and generosity of a great king.

Tamaahmaah explained that his visit was an informal one—he had come simply to welcome Vancouver as an old friend and to invite his ships into the bay. Vancouver was cautious. He told the King he had sent Whidbey to examine another anchorage nearby and his decision would depend on this report. Meanwhile he entertained his guests royally, giving them rich presents and watching with pleasure the obvious affection between Tamaahmaah and his young wife. Tahowmannoo was a very beautiful and lively girl of about sixteen, a favourite daughter of Kahowmotoo. The King constantly held her hands and caressed her without the least embarrassment as they sat in the cabin—by European standards, Vancouver thought, trying to be severe, it was a little extravagant and perhaps undignified; but no one could help enjoying the sight of two people so obviously happy together, and the simpler ways of the island people made it all quite natural and proper.

It was soon clear that Tamaahmaah had no intention of pressing Vancouver to trade him firearms; he promised that everything the ships needed would be delivered promptly and in an orderly way, under his own absolute control instead of by individual bartering. Vancouver also learned by discreet questions that there were no cannons in the bay and when Whidbey came back with an unfavourable report of the other anchorage, he gladly accepted Tamaahmaah's repeated invitations to come into Karakakoa.

The ships moved into the bay next morning and were met by thousands of canoes, most of them anxious to trade. But Vancouver allowed no one aboard and no trading of any kind until he had secured his ships for what he expected to be a fairly long stay. The moment the anchors were down, eleven very large canoes, each driven by 36 paddles, put out from shore. They were in arrow-head formation, perfectly spaced in two slanting lines from the lead canoe. In the bow of the lead canoe stood Tamaahmaah, his arms folded, his face proud and impassive. From his massive shoulders a cloak of brilliant yellow feathers dropped like a cascade to touch the narrow deck at his heels; from time to time it gleamed in the sunlight as the King moved one or other of his arms to change the direction of his racing escort.

The canoes made a complete circuit of the ships, changing formation several times with all the precision of a battle fleet, then stopped in line abreast squarely across the stern of the ship and at some distance behind it. From there Tamaahmaah's canoe shot suddenly forward, driven by the full power of eighteen strong men on each side, and stopped dead in the water exactly alongside the *Discovery*'s gangway. Tamaahmaah stepped lightly over and climbed aboard.

His greeting to Vancouver was completely formal, as though they had never seen each other before. Taking him by the hand, he asked if he and his men were true friends. When Vancouver said: yes, they were, Tamaahmaah said he understood the ships and the people in them belonged to King George. Was King George a good friend? Again Vancouver said: yes. Tamaahmaah struck his great chest with his free hand. "I, too, am a firm, good friend," he said, then leaned forward and rubbed noses with Vancouver. A moment later he turned and, with a regal gesture, summoned the remaining canoes alongside. Each held a gift of ten fat hogs, and a swarm of smaller canoes followed with fresh vegetables and native cloth and mats and other gifts. Vancouver was deeply impressed by the royal scale of Tamaahmaah's generosity and still more deeply touched by his sincere and evident desire for friendship and understanding.

The ships stayed on in the bay for over two weeks, while the small boats went out to survey the coast of the island

and Menzies made an expedition into the interior. Vancouver worked steadily to increase Tamaahmaah's power and prestige among his people and to incline him towards peace and good government. He quickly became aware of the jealousy of the other chiefs. Even Kahowmotoo complained that Vancouver was favouring the King in his attentions and his gifts. Tianna, a chief as powerful as Kahowmotoo but a young man, surly and savage, was openly hostile to Tamaahmaah; the King, in return, hated him so powerfully that he turned abruptly away whenever Tianna spoke and his face took on the ferocious and terrifying look that Vancouver remembered from so many years before.

Vancouver met the situation directly and firmly. He was fair and generous with Kahowmotoo and Tianna, but whenever they protested some favour shown to Tamaahmaah he reminded them that they were chiefs under the King; they should be thankful, he said, for the good things that were done for them and not jealous of Tamaahmaah's greater position. And he continued to emphasize at every opportunity the superior rank and authority of the King.

This was easily done, because the people were very quick to notice and recognize every special attention. Almost daily Vancouver visited Tamaahmaah ashore, always with a guard of honour of marines in full dress uniform. He had his sail-makers make a full suit of sails for the King's largest canoe and rigged it with a Union Jack and a special royal pennant. Tamaahmaah came frequently aboard the *Discovery*, where he was ceremoniously received. The King gave a display in Vancouver's honour, ending it with a mock battle in which he and his boldest warriors took part. Vancouver at once ordered a magnificent display of fireworks in return, and the people came from all over the island to see it.

The mock battle gave Vancouver a good chance to judge Tamaahmaah's vigour and prowess. It was a violent and dangerous affair, fought under formal rules but otherwise with little regard for safety except that the heavy throwing spears had blunted points. Many warriors were knocked unconscious and dragged off the field as though dead. The King took part in the later stages and at once became the main object of attack by the opposing side. In one incident six powerful men launched their spears against him at the same moment. Tamaahmaah caught three of them in mid air in his left hand, broke two others against his own spear and moved his great body slightly to let the sixth pass harmlessly by.

Such a man, Vancouver knew, was bound to look upon real warfare as the readiest means of proving his power and greatness. He worked against this by appealing to Tamaahmaah's own wisdom and genuine concern for his people's welfare, and by balancing the maturity and wisdom of Kahowmotoo, who was ready to accept peace, against the warlike ambitions of the fiercely jealous Tianna. Shortly before the ships were ready to leave, Tamaahmaah and Kahowmotoo told Vancouver they would follow his advice and accept any honourable arrangement he could make for peace in the nearby islands.

The day before the ships left, Tamaahmaah came aboard *Discovery* to give Vancouver a magnificent cloak of red and yellow feathers. Then he brought out the cloak of yellow feathers he had worn to welcome them to his island and dropped its gleaming folds in the brilliant sunlight.

This, he said, was his gift to King George. He showed Vancouver two holes behind the shoulders, made by an enemy spear in the last great battle he had fought for conquest of the island. Then, carefully and reverently, he folded it again. No one but he had ever worn it, Tamaahmaah said; and no other man must dare touch it to his shoulders until it reached King George.

# 16. The Second Summer

FROM Hawaii Vancouver took his ships on to the island of Maui, where he was greeted by the chiefs Titeere and Taio. Titeere, the supreme chief, was an old man, worn and wrinkled by his great age, by the bitter wars he had fought and by constant use of a native drug. But he was still quick-witted and intelligent and his authority was great though his islands, like himself, were ravaged and impoverished by the wars.

Taio was still young, but he too was worn by the wars and by excessive use of the drug. He still remembered and cherished the close friendship he had formed with Vancouver when the islands were first discovered; in proof of it, he brought a lock of Vancouver's hair, decorated with tiny scarlet feathers, which he had kept safely among his most precious possessions through all the years since Cook's last voyage.

Both chiefs knew Vancouver had come to find out about the deaths of Hergest and Gooch and the able seaman of the *Daedalus*. But Vancouver spoke to them first of peace and of restoring the prosperity of the islands. They accepted his reasoning at once, but explained that Tamaahmaah was not to be trusted. He would make peace only to attack them when they were off guard. Taio then asked if Vancouver was really sincere in his advice. All the traders who came to the islands said exactly the opposite, urging them to make war and willingly supplying firearms. Vancouver smiled. The traders, he explained, encouraged them to make war because they wanted to sell arms, not because they thought wars were good for the islanders. Taio understood at once. As for any treachery by Tamaahmaah, Vancouver went on, he would tell the King that he must accept whatever peace terms were agreed upon or lose his friendship. This impressed the two chiefs and Taio said that when Vancouver returned the following winter they would go with him to meet Tamaahmaah.

Vancouver then asked them directly: what bad thing had Lieutenant Hergest and Mr. Gooch done that they deserved to be killed?

They had done nothing, Titeere answered. The killing had been done by evil men, when no chiefs were present. Three of the murderers had been put to death for the crime, but four others had escaped to the hills. These were now back at their own village in the island of Oahu. Tomohomoho, Titeere's brother, would go with Vancouver and arrange for their punishment.

At Oahu three of the four men were quickly found and brought aboard under arrest. Tomohomoho and Tennaree, the local chief, were fully satisfied of their guilt and wanted to execute them immediately. But Vancouver was afraid that they might be innocent men, selected by jealousy or prejudice, and insisted upon holding a formal trial and hearing as many witnesses as could be found. When their guilt was proved beyond all doubt, the native people were summoned from the village. Hundreds came off in their canoes and held silently beside the *Discovery* while the details of the crime and sentence were read out to them in their own language. Then the murderers were put in irons and handed over to their own chief, Tennaree. Tennaree took them one by one into a canoe tied alongside the *Discovery* and blew out their brains with a pistol. It was a grim and shocking lesson, deliberately planned to warn the islanders that such wanton crimes would not be easily forgiven or forgotten.

*Discovery* and *Chatham* went on to Kauai, the northern-most of the principal islands, but it was now the middle of March and Vancouver sent *Chatham* ahead to the north-west coast, so that she would have time to make necessary repairs at Nootka. At the end of the month *Discovery* followed, and after a long and stormy voyage, rejoined her in Fitzhugh Sound late in May.

From Fitzhugh Sound northward far into Alaska, the Pacific Coast is shielded from the ocean by a succession of large islands. Behind these the coast-line itself is broken by long inlets every bit as complicated as those behind Vancouver Island. This was the principal country of the fur-traders, where sea-otters were abundant and Indian tribes were numerous. A few parts of it had been roughly charted, either by the Spaniards or by traders, but little was really known of it and few of the inlets had been penetrated by white men. It was work for the small boats again, under all the same difficulties as the previous season, but in a colder, rainier climate.

The work started at once and by June 2nd, Johnstone had reached the head of Dean Channel in the cutter while Vancouver in the yawl, following the other side of King Island, found his marks there a day or so later. Even as they turned back, another great explorer was struggling overland from the east towards the same point. Some six weeks later, Alexander Mackenzie reached salt water at the head of Dean Channel, the first man in history to cross Canada from Atlantic to Pacific.

The small boats worked on, under Puget and Johnstone and Whidbey, under Vancouver himself and Spelman Swaine. They were hard driven, because Vancouver knew that neither his ships nor his men could stand more than one full season's work after this; and there was still a weary length of coast-line ahead, reaching northward into colder and harder country, where the work would go always more slowly. But if he could not spare his men, Vancouver did what he could to make them more comfortable by ordering special rations to permit two hot meals a day on all the boat trips, with an extra issue of grog to be used whenever the officer commanding the expedition thought it was needed. And he bore his own share of exposure and hardship through some of the longest trips of the season, though he was already a sick man, under constant treatment from Menzies.

The task of moving the ships up from station to station along the narrow passages inside the islands was almost as arduous as were the boat explorations. It was seldom possible to sail, which meant hour upon hour of rowing for the weary men at the oars, often against strong tides. Good anchorage was difficult to find on the steeply shelving, rocky bottom; and usually it was necessary to carry lines ashore to keep the ships from swinging and sliding the anchors into deep water. Ropes and cables were rotten from long usage, and several of the anchors broke because they were poorly made.

In the end, rather than struggle up the long narrow reach of Grenville Channel, which Whidbey had already explored as far as the mouth of the Skeena River, Vancouver decided to take his ships outside Banks Island. The Spanish charts showed a clear passage through to the mainland just north of the Skeena and it would be easy to pick up the mainland shore again and carry it on from there.

The ships sailed into the strait on a southeast gale, late in the afternoon of July 20th. Almost at once they were among rocky islets and reefs and ledges, with the weather thickening and the gale increasing. Vancouver chose to hold on rather than turn back, only to find the channel more and more broken, with the surf foaming against hidden rocks on every side. It quickly became impossible to turn back, and he dared not anchor without some shelter from the increasing gale. Yet only an hour of hazy daylight was left. After that not even the best eyes or the finest seamanship would take them through. They would have to trust to faulty anchors and rotting cables to hold somehow against the heave of the swells and the increasing power of the gale.

Then, out of the scudding mists, in that dismal sea where they knew they were all alone, an English whaleboat came pulling towards them, riding the crests, sliding down the swells, until she was close enough to signal them to follow. Half an hour later they were anchored in a sheltered cove near the *Butterworth* of London and two other small trading-vessels. Captain Brown of the *Butterworth* saluted the naval ships with seven guns and Vancouver returned the compliment with five guns. But if this acknowledgement was restrained by naval rules, Captain Brown was royally and thankfully welcomed aboard *Discovery* when he came over a few minutes later.

The *Butterworth* had hit a rock in finding her way into the anchorage a few days earlier, but the damage was now almost repaired and in the meanwhile the two smaller ships had been out in search of furs. Captain Brown said he had found a large opening to the northward and beyond it the entrance to a still larger opening, in which the Indians told him they travelled sometimes for three months to trade with other Indians. He had turned back because the Indians of one village had attempted to attack and forced him to fire on them.

To Vancouver this was important news. They were near the latitude shown for the Strait of de Fonte in some of the Spanish charts, and the Indian story aroused new hope of a passage inland through the mountain ranges. The next day, in good weather, he moved his ships and on July 23rd came to a safe anchorage in Observatory Inlet, near the present boundary between Alaska and British Columbia. From there he started out in the yawl, with Puget in the launch, on the longest and hardest boat journey of the season.

Early in the trip, when they were still exploring the long reach of Portland Canal, they met with Indians who were different from any they had known before. There were fifteen or twenty of them in two canoes, the larger of which was steered by a very ugly old woman with a great protruding lip ornament that added to her unpleasant appearance. The men were well built and powerful, but with fierce, unyielding faces made more terrifying by streaks of red and black and white paint. They were armed with sixteen-foot spears, well-made bows and a few muskets. Each wore a short dagger on a lanyard round his neck, sheathed on his chest, and a protective cloak of tough animal hides, sewn on the right shoulder and down the left side under the armpit, but open on the right side so that both arms were free for action.

This formidable crew approached the boats with spears and other weapons laid ready in the canoes. Vancouver met them calmly, offering the usual presents, but the Indians contemptuously refused them. The old woman talked constantly in a scolding, angry voice. Once she spoke sharply to the man in the bow of the canoe. He straightened instantly in his seat and moved his long spears so that they were evenly divided, six or eight on each side of him, all pointing threateningly forward. A moment later he leapt up, pulled on his war cloak, drew his dagger and scowled menacingly at the men in the boat. Again Vanouver watched calmly, measuring the meaning of the action. In spite of all the hostile preparations and the ferocity of the threat, the canoe was too far away for any immediate attack; he decided they wanted to show they were on guard and ready to fight back. He kept his boats together and his men steady and continued on his way.

The canoes followed. The men in them now waved a few inferior skins of sea-otter and kept shouting "winnee watter", which meant "stop and trade". But they still refused to accept blue cloth or iron or copper or any other goods the white men offered. In a little while they went away, then came swiftly back, singing loudly and with their arms laid aside. They traded at once, willingly and cheerfully, for the very goods they had just refused so contemptuously. When there was nothing more to trade one or two of them attempted to steal small articles out of the boats, so Vancouver ordered them off. They went reluctantly, but peacefully.

All this was just one more in the hundreds of minor incidents with Indian people that had filled the two long summers in the inside waters. Officers and men discussed it as the boats rowed along, comparing it with other incidents, trying to guess at what it all meant. A few thought that these might have been the Indians fired upon by Captain Brown; others thought the boats might have been too slow in offering to trade; Vancouver believed the Indians wanted arms and ammunition and had been willing to trade for other goods only when they realized no firearms would be offered. Like so many other incidents, friendly as well as hostile, it remained a mystery because neither side could speak the other's language.

During the next few days, as they completed the exploration of Portland Canal and rounded into Behm's Canal, the boats met with other parties of Indians. Some were friendly or even timid. Others, fully armed and apparently commanded by the wizened, shrewish old women who steered the canoes, were surly and threatening; but the calmness and steady discipline of the boats' crews, with the usual friendly offer of a few small gifts, always broke down the hostility and there was no attack.

On August 11th, already fourteen days away from the ships, they reached the mouth of the Unuk River, where salmon were running in enormous numbers. The men waded out eagerly and speared them with boat-hooks, because provisions were already short. But spawning was far advanced and they were poor eating. Menzies called them "hunchbacked salmon" from the high, gristly hump on the backs of the males and guessed that they died immediately after spawning, for the river-banks and the nearby shores below highwater mark were scattered with thousands of dead fish.

Beyond the Unuk River the canal turned westward through Behm's narrows, then southward towards the ships, widening as it went. Almost at once the boats met with more Indians, who put off from shore in four canoes, two of them very large and one of these, as usual, steered by an ugly old hag with a very large oval of polished wood wedged between her gums and her protruding lower lip. In spite of this warning sign, these Indians appeared more than usually friendly. They met the yawl first and traded happily, repeating the word "wacon", meaning "friendship", over and over again. Then the two larger canoes made off towards the launch, which was some distance away.

Feeling perfectly secure, Vancouver took the yawl into shore and, leaving Puget in charge, climbed up on some rocks to take compass bearings. While he was still there he heard the natives making a great deal of noise and calling out to their friends in the two large canoes. When he got back to the yawl he saw they were clustered closely round it and the two large canoes were just coming in. Puget quickly told him the Indians were trying to steal from the boat and seemed likely to make trouble. Vancouver jumped in and ordered the yawl out from shore.

The Indians ashore got back in their canoes and grabbed

hold of the stern of the boat, but the men had the oars out quickly and began to pull away. Just then the largest of the canoes, steered by the old woman, cut across the bow of the yawl and the old woman herself snatched the head-line and made the canoe fast to the boat. Almost in the same instant a young chief swung himself on to the bow of the yawl and sat there cross-legged pulling a painted wolf mask over his face. Still another Indian reached in and snatched a loaded musket from near the bow.

Vancouver knew the situation was desperate. The men in the yawl were hopelessly outnumbered and all the weapons but two or three muskets, a blunderbuss and a shotgun were still in the arms chest. He glanced towards the launch and saw it was still too far away to help. There was nothing to do but talk and gain time while the launch came up. As the young chief leapt aboard, every man in the canoes had taken up his arms and a forest of long spears pointed inwards from every direction against the men in the yawl. Vancouver moved slowly forward, a musket ready in his hands. He spoke quietly and politely to the young chief, asking him to get back into his canoe. The young man stood up, signing that his men would put down their spears if Vancouver would drop his musket. Without hesitation, Vancouver did so. The spears were lowered and the young chief stepped back into the canoe.

Immediately the old woman in the stern began scolding and driving the men to attack, with an unceasing torrent of bitter words. Daggers leapt from their sheaths again and fifty spears pointed inboard from all directions against the men in the yawl. At the stern, an old man in a smaller canoe screamed and scolded as fiercely as the old woman; spears were thrust out, passing within inches of the men at the oars. Vancouver moved back among them, still calm, still signalling for peace. The spears dropped as he approached, only to be taken up again as he passed. The old man moved his canoe in and seized the oars on the starboard side. Indians reached into the yawl and began to steal everything they could lay their hands on.

Vancouver glanced again at the launch and judged it now within range. Quietly, still hoping to avoid the attack that would overwhelm them almost instantly, he ordered his men to fire the few weapons left to them. At his order a young Indian in one of the canoes leapt to his feet and pointed his musket at Vancouver's chest. Vancouver heard the hammer snap in a misfire and in the next moment the ragged volley from his own men sounded, followed by heavier fire from the launch.

Instead of attacking, the Indians jumped overboard, tilting their canoes as a shield against the fire, and began paddling as fast as they could for shore. Vancouver ordered the arms chest broken open and started in instant pursuit. Then he found that two of his men, Robert Betton and George Bridgeman, had been seriously wounded by spear thrusts. Betton, reaching for the arms chest, had parried one blow with his hands, but a second thrust had driven into his thigh and he was bleeding seriously; Bridgeman, also pierced through the thigh from side to side, was in better condition, but still needed immediate attention.

The launch came up and Menzies was soon at work on the wounded men. With the bleeding stopped and the wounds bound up, both were wrapped up in blankets and made as comfortable as possible, one in each boat. For a moment, Vancouver considered going ashore to destroy the canoes. But several Indians had fallen in the volleys from the boats and their companions could now be heard, well back in the woods, wailing over the bodies. Further punishment would mean little. Too much, Vancouver felt, had been done already. He blamed himself for being trapped into such a deadly situation, knowing well that the long series of happy encounters with the native peoples had led to a false sense of security and relaxed the precautions he had insisted on at the start of the voyage. He even found excuses for the Indians; more than one of them had told of trading with other Europeans for muskets that blew up at the first charge. But he could not forgive the treachery of their friendly approach; he named the bay they had come from Traitor's Cove and the place where the attack had been made Escape Point.

Since Menzies said the wounded men were comfortable, Vancouver continued his survey with as much care and thoroughness as ever, searching out a safe way to bring the ships forward. By the time he got back to his base at Salmon Cove in Observatory Inlet the boats had been out for twenty-three days, travelling seven hundred miles to cover only some sixty miles of direct travel northward. In spite of short rations and cramped quarters, the wounded men were well on the way to recovery.

# 17. King-Maker and Peace-Maker

THE ships moved forward to two more stations, Port Stewart, almost opposite Traitor's Cove and Port Protection at the north end of Prince of Wales Island; but by mid-September the weather was so bad that work in the small boats became impossible and the season's exploration ended at Cape Decision, the southern point of Kuiu Island.

It was a grand relief to get back to the open sea and Vancouver turned his thoughts again to the problems of dealing with the Spaniards. He expected new orders from England by the *Daedalus* and earnestly hoped to bring the affair to a successful conclusion.

But the *Daedalus* was not at Nootka when he arrived there and the Spanish commander of the port had no new instructions, so the ships sailed for California after two or three days. They met with *Daedalus* along the coast between San Francisco and Monterey, but she brought no further orders from England. The Admiralty, it seemed, had forgotten the King's Commissioner and his little expedition in the faraway north Pacific. Bitterly disappointed and denied the hospitality of the Spanish ports by the new commandant, Señor Arrillaga, Vancouver followed the coast to 30°N., then turned towards the Hawaiian Islands, where he felt he could at least be sure of courtesy and hospitality.

The three ships reached Hawaii early in January of 1794 and were warmly welcomed by King Tamaahmaah, who put out to them from Whyeatea Bay. This, he said, was his favourite part of the island and he begged the ships to anchor there.

Vancouver was delighted to see his old friend again and at once sent Whidbey in to look over the anchorage. Whidbey soon came back with word that the bay had no protection at all from the northerly winds, which blew almost constantly at that time of year, so Vancouver decided he would have to go on to Karakakoa Bay. He asked Tamaahmaah to go with him, but the King said that was impossible; he was bound by taboos to stay at Whyeatea for several more days. Vancouver, anxious to get a quick start on the provisioning and refitting of his ships, pressed Tamaahmaah to come. "It is impossible," Tamaahmaah said. "A king is the last person who should break the established laws of his land."

As always where the good of his ships and his mission was concerned, Vancouver was relentless. Knowing how Tamaahmaah valued it, he appealed to their friendship. Surely this wasn't much to ask. If Tamaahmaah refused, it must be because his friendship had weakened.

The King withdrew into dignified, unhappy silence for several hours, refusing to eat or talk with Vancouver. At last he agreed to send his half-brother ashore to the priests to ask permission to leave Whyeatea, but he reproached Vancouver for doubting his friendship. Vancouver would soon see, he promised, how powerful and sincere that friendship was. With this, the King's cheerfulness returned. He ate a huge breakfast and settled himself comfortably aboard the *Discovery* for the voyage to Karakakoa.

Vancouver noticed that Tamaahmaah had not brought Tahowmannoo, his favourite wife, aboard with him. He soon learned that she and Tamaahmaah had quarrelled and separated, and that Tahowmannoo was in Karakakoa with her father, Kahowmotoo. The separation distressed Vancouver because of his real affection for Tamaahmaah and the pleasure he had felt at seeing the devotion of the royal couple the year before, but he was concerned, too, about the political meaning of the separation. Kahowmotoo was a great and important chief, at least the equal of the jealous Tianna and inferior only to Tamaahmaah himself. Without his support, Tamaahmaah might not be able to maintain supreme power and the island would be plunged again into destructive warfare.

Vancouver made discreet and careful inquiries from the other chiefs aboard and soon learned that the trouble between the two was a misunderstanding rather than a real quarrel. Both Tamaahmaah and the Queen were willing to forgive each other, but pride prevented either of them from admitting it. So he went directly to the King and asked if he could help bring the two of them together again. Tamaahmaah listened to the request with great dignity and thanked him courteously. He was happy, he said, to have Vancouver's advice at any time on political or public affairs. But his private affairs were his own and he would manage them himself. Vancouver accepted this firm refusal in silence. But he did not give up hope.

When the ships anchored in Karakakoa Bay they were greeted by tremendous cheering from great crowds of the islanders along the shores and in their canoes. Tamaahmaah at once took over the whole organization of supplying the ships, the observatory was set up in its usual place and Menzies took an expedition ashore to climb the volcano Mauna Loa. Everything was as it had been a year before except for the cloud that hung over the love of the King and Queen.

Vancouver soon learned that Tamaahmaah was hoping to build a small ship in the harbour. An English seaman named Boid had been left ashore by the *Lady Washington* to help him with this venture. Vancouver talked with Boid and found him a good man, hard-working and skilful, but not trained in shipbuilding. So he sent his own carpenters ashore to lay the ship's keel and build the frame. They worked so well that before the time came to leave the little man-of-war was finished to the point where Boid could safely take charge. Vancouver supplied all the metal fittings for the ship, oakum and pitch for caulking, the masts for a sloop rig and a full set of sails.

With all these affairs going smoothly ahead, Vancouver turned again to his diplomatic efforts. He knew now that he wanted not only peace among the islands, but a strong political union in the main island under Tamaahmaah and a protective arrangement for all the islands with Great Britain. And the necessary first step to these arrangements was an affectionate reunion between Tamaahmaah and Tahowmannoo.

Vancouver had learned that Tamaahmaah had refused

not only his own offer to help, but similar offers from all his chiefs and advisers; so there was now no one to whom he could turn for help. He took the chance of offending the King by again offering his services. This time the offer was promptly and gratefully accepted. Tamaahmaah explained that he could not have accepted such a suggestion from one of his chiefs, or gone to any of them himself, without offending all the others. So Vancouver had given him hope where there had seemed to be none. But Vancouver must understand, he went on, that the King could make no concessions to his wife, nor must it appear that he had taken any smallest active step towards the reunion.

Vancouver at once proposed a plan. Tamaahmaah slapped his huge thighs and roared with laughter when he heard it. Then he found a flaw. How, if he played his part in it, could he know in advance whether or not the Queen would accept a reconciliation? Vancouver gave him two pieces of paper and told him to mark one to show that the Queen was willing, the other that she was not. The right paper would be delivered to him when the time came, and he would know how to act.

The next day the Queen and all her relatives and follow-ers were invited aboard the *Discovery*. Tamaahmaah was not. Vancouver entertained them royally and soon the party was very gay. When everyone was laughing and joking and admiring the fine gifts that had been given out with great freedom, Vancouver drew attention to Tamaahmaah's absence. Wouldn't it be a fine joke, he suggested, to send him an old scrap of paper wrapped in a huge package to look like a handsome gift? Everyone agreed it was a wonderful idea. So Vancouver carefully wrapped the paper that showed the Queen was willing and

sent it ashore with great ceremony to Tamaahmaah.

The King played his part perfectly. He opened the package immediately and worked through all the wrappings until he came to the piece of paper. He waved it in the air, calling on everyone to come and see the splendid gift his friend Vancouver had sent him. The joke seemed just as fine to them as it had to the people aboard the *Discovery*. Tamaahmaah shook with laughter and perhaps also with happiness at the secret message marked on the paper. He must go out at once, he roared, and thank his good friend Vancouver for remembering him so generously.

Aboard the ship he forced his way through the crowd, still shouting that he must hurry to thank Vancouver for remembering him. He burst into the cabin, then stopped dead, staring at his Queen in pretended amazement. A moment later, he started to back out of the door. But Vancouver stopped him, took him gently by the arm and led him forward. He lifted the Queen's hand and placed it in Tamaahmaah's. For a moment the two stood in silence, then they embraced and wept.

At rest in his mind, Tamaahmaah turned readily to the other great matters of state. He called in his chiefs from all over the island and they came, bringing their people, until there were several thousand camped along the shores of the bay. The council of chiefs and priests met daily to discuss the proposals, to question Vancouver and put forward ideas of their own. There were solemn ceremonies at the great temple in which all the leaders, including Vancouver and some of his officers, took part. The islanders put on magnificent entertainments of singing and acting and dancing and the ships gave displays of fireworks in return. And gradually the great plan was worked out.

There was a final meeting aboard *Discovery* on February 25th. All the ships' officers and Lieutenant Puget of the *Chatham* were present, with Tamaahmaah and all his principal chiefs. Tamaahmaah opened the discussion with a powerful speech explaining all the reasons for his voluntary surrender to Great Britain. The purpose was order and protection, so that the island peoples could develop and trade peacefully with European ships, without fear of direct conquest by white men or hazard of the evil habits of the traders, who often swindled them with inferior goods or left without paying for supplies and services. But internal sovereignty would remain with the King, the chiefs, and the islanders themselves. There was to be no interference, even by the British, with the religious, political or economic life of the islands.

When he was finished each chief spoke in turn, and each had something useful to add. Kahowmotoo, who wanted to be King of Maui under Tamaahmaah, hoped that final conquest of the island would not be laid aside in the new plan. Karaheero, chief of Kau, said that he was completely satisfied and would bring the full support of his people. Tianna, no longer surly and difficult now that Tamaahmaah's power was firmly established, agreed with the others but wanted a British ship and a British garrison established in the islands for their protection. He added the practical suggestion that any ship sent out must have in it some of the officers of *Discovery* or *Chatham* so that the natives could tell it from an American, French or Spanish vessel.

The assembly then, still in the cabin under *Discovery*'s quarter-deck, declared that they were no longer people of Hawaii, but people of Britain. They moved out on deck and repeated this announcement to the people in the canoes massed about the ship, who took it up in turn with a great shout that was repeated again all along the crowded beaches.

Puget went ashore with a guard of honour and hoisted the Union Jack in the brilliant sunshine. As the flag broke, the ships fired a salute. And on shore the ship's metal workers went up to fix a great copper plate in the solid rock, recording that on this day the island had been ceded to Great Britain with full ceremony and the approval of King Tamaahmaah, his chiefs, his priests and all his people.

A few days later Vancouver said sad and final farewells to Tamaahmaah and all the many other friends he had won for himself and his nation in the islands. The crowds of people along the shore gently and silently melted away into the back country from which they had come. Tamaahmaah, who had been kept ashore by taboos and religious ceremonies, asked Vancouver to delay for one more day so that they could spend it together. He and Tahowmannoo came aboard and stayed on until the last sad moment before the ships left.

As he sailed from the island and set course for the northwest coast again, Vancouver regretted that neither time nor the condition of his ships would allow him to go on to the other islands and arrange for the peace among them that he believed was so necessary. But he had already gone far beyond his orders and he could only hope that Tamaahmaah's obvious power and authority would now quickly establish peace.

In fact, this was exactly what happened. Tamaahmaah conquered the nearby islands in the following year; his power grew steadily and he ruled wisely until his death in 1819, to become the greatest figure in Hawaiian history. Knowing that his son, Tamaahmaah II, was a weak man, the King named Tahowmannoo, whom he had loved devotedly from the time of their reunion aboard *Discovery*, to be Regent. Tahowmannoo became a Christian in 1825 and continued to rule the islands wisely and well until her death in 1832. The Tamaahmaah or Kamehameha dynasty as it later became, founded on strong and truly great people, continued to be a force for good until the death of Kamehameha V nearly a hundred years after the first discovery of the islands by Captain Cook.

# 18. Close of the Great Survey

THE two ships became separated in rough weather a few days after leaving the Hawaiian Islands. Vancouver shortened *Discovery*'s sail to wait for his slower consort, but *Chatham* did not catch up. Puget was struggling with four feet of water in the hold, shipped through leaks above the water-line. Long before the ship was dry and sailing easily again, all hope of catching *Discovery* was gone.

*Discovery* held on towards the prearranged meeting-place at Cook's River, in Alaska, and arrived there in April, 1794. Vancouver had decided to start the summer's work at 60 ° N., the northern limit of his orders, and work back down the coast to tie into his previous summer's work at Cape Decision.

He was only thirty-six years old, but he was a sick man, already suffering from tuberculosis, though he did not know it. His ships and all their rigging and equipment were badly worn, but he had to nurse them somehow through this summer of hard and dangerous work and through the long voyage home by Cape Horn. His officers and men, young and healthy though nearly all of them were, were weary and worn by three years at sea. Another summer of exposure in the small boats, of hunger and cold and wet, of danger from the sea and uncertain-tempered Indian bands, must have seemed almost beyond endurance. Yet discipline and seamanship remained perfect and every man aboard turned to the work with the same devotion and drive he had shown in the first season, and with the skill earned by two seasons of hard experience. Vancouver looked at his people with pity for the weariness he knew they must feel and love for the loyalty they had shown him; he worried about the wretched state of his ships; his sickness made him irritable and prevented him from taking active part in the small boat explorations. But at no time did he have any least thought of turning back for England until the last indentation of the coast-line had been probed and the existence or otherwise of a northwest passage was finally proved.

Cook's River, nearly sixty miles wide at the entrance, was the great inlet into which Cook had sailed for two hundred miles without finding an end. Cook himself had believed he was very near the end of it, but in spite of this it remained the most likely chance of a passage.

It was still bitterly cold when *Discovery* sailed along Kodiak Island and into Cook's River. Ice was solid on her rigging and her sails were stiff and hard to handle. Snow blizzards blew down on her from the barren hills and sudden fierce winds strained at her weakened masts and rotting cordage. Vancouver had to use every art of seamanship to make his way up the inlet, sailing whenever the wind was fair, day or night, sometimes trusting his ship to drift with the tide, often taking her across extensive sand-bars that were dotted with great round rocks carried down by the glaciers. Several times the ships grounded and the seamen had to carry out lines and anchors in the bitter weather to haul her free; many of them were suffering from frost-bite and the weather continued so cold that even brief spells of sunshine did not warm it noticeably.

Again and again Vancouver remembered making the same long, difficult journey with Cook; here the *Resolution* had grounded, here she had sailed freely between two long sand-bars, here she had anchored in safety from the tearing run of the flood-tide. Finally he passed beyond Cook's last anchorage and took his ships even beyond the farthest reach of the *Resolution*'s small boats. But in the end he was forced to anchor just as the tide slackened among the confusion of rocks and sand-bars in Turnagain Arm; and almost as soon as the anchors were out the wind fell away to nothing.

Whidbey went away at once in one of the small boats to find the end of the arm or search out a way for the ships. Then, as the ebb-tide increased its flow, great broken chunks and masses of ice came grinding and pounding down against the ship. Fifteen or twenty frightened natives came alongside in a big skin canoe and asked to be allowed to stay aboard until the tide turned and the danger lessened; they were unarmed and very quiet and orderly, so Vancouver welcomed them and hoisted their canoe out of danger. Then a heavy mass of ice broke the small bower-anchor cable and left the ship to swing on the best bower-cable alone, which fortunately was new and unusually heavy. But the ice bumped and crashed against the bow and the sides of the ship and no one knew what damage was being done or whether the single cable would stand the masses that pressed against it, in spite of its strength and thickness.

Vancouver had hoped that the returning flood would ease things, but it simply brought the ice masses back in greater force than ever, pounding the ship with shock after shock that threatened to tear away her planks or bring down the masts. So it continued for two or three days, while the men worked as best they could in slack-water periods to recover the anchor and Vancouver worried for Whidbey's safety. The anchor was the third they had lost since entering the inlet and stocks were so low that they could not afford to be without it. On the second day they managed to hook up the broken cable with a drag and tie it to a buoy, but the ice drove them off before they could do more.

On that same slack-water another group of natives, with several Russian traders, came off to seek the sanctuary of the ship. Vancouver welcomed them as he had the others and the Russians told him by signs that the arm ended in a shallow river only ten or twelve miles away. They became very nervous as the tide began to run and the ice battered the ship again. One tried to look down in the hold to see if the ship was making water. Another insisted that the pumps should be working. Vancouver tried to explain that the ship had withstood the battering of the ice for several days and was making no water; but as soon as there was a clear lane through the ice towards shore they asked for their canoe to be hoisted overboard and paddled swiftly away for the greater security of dry land.

The lost anchor was recovered on the next slack and a little breeze came up, so Vancouver decided to move his ship. She went aground almost at once and hung there, heeling awkwardly, until the flood-tide floated her again. On the next slack he moved into mid-channel and found safe anchorage in twelve fathoms over sandy bottom. Then the weather changed from the cold bright days to mist and rain, clearing again the following day. The flow of ice slackened and the small boats went ashore again to get water and fuel. In the evening Whidbey returned safely after a week of many dangers to report that the arm ended as the Russians had said and that there was no safe passage for the ship beyond her present anchorage.

*Chatham* rejoined *Discovery* at the head of Cook's Inlet after Vancouver had made a four-day trip in the yawl to test the last remaining arm, which ended, as the others had, in a sandy river—the Matanuska. The two ships then turned back down the long, unfriendly inlet to continue the summer's work.

There was little enough of summer in the weather as they worked southward through the rest of May and June. *Discovery* struggled along the Kenai Peninsula through battering storms that broke her bowsprit. Passing behind Montague Island she was almost capsized by a sudden, savage flurry of wind that funnelled through a gap in the mountains; it was all over in a few minutes, but by then her sails were split and her foreyard broken. Vancouver took her on into Chalmers harbour, farther along the big island, and sent his carpenters ashore to make a new foreyard and bowsprit, while Whidbey and Johnstone went off in the small boats to explore the dozen arms and inlets that open into Prince William Sound.

The weather was milder now, but very stormy. Great slides of rock and snow and ice rumbled down the steep mountains in every direction. A strong gale, with cold, heavy rain, blew in from the northeast, soaking the carpenters at their work and making Vancouver worry again for the safety of his boats' crews. On June 1st a fierce gale from due east broke another anchor cable and the ship swung aground on the change of the tide; but once again she came off undamaged. The following morning Whidbey came back, bringing a seaman who had been injured by a rock from a slide that swept down into the sea not a hundred yards from where they were camped. He left the injured man, took on extra supplies and went off again immediately.

Towards the middle of June, Johnstone and Whidbey completed the survey of Prince William Sound and Vancouver took his ship thankfully southward to rejoin *Chatham* in Yakutat Bay. From there the two ships followed the long curve of the coast-line down to Cross Sound at 58°N. They were now back among the complicated series of islands in which they had completed the previous summer's work. This, the crews knew, was the last chance of finding a passage and winning the reward of £20,000 that had for so long been offered by the British government. It was a slender hope, but they clung to it as men will; and whether they found it or not, the end of the enormous task was in sight. A few more days or weeks would bring them in sight of islands and passages they had worked in the previous year. After that they would leave the cold, harsh northern country and the constant risk of inshore sailing. Every league under the ships' keels would be a league towards homes they had not seen in four long years.

George Vancouver, who understood better than any man how tightly he had stretched the endurance of his people and his ships, felt a sharp anxiety about this final stage of the exploration. In spite of the unyielding determination with which he had sought for it, he had never really believed in the northwest passage; he had expected only to check every possibility to its final end against the feet of the mountains, and so prove that Cook's judgment was sound. It had been far more painful and difficult and exhausting than he had expected, and on the spread of the master charts that Baker worked over so steadily he could see what a formidable achievement it was. Only a short gap now remained, less than two degrees of latitude. But he knew, only too well, what perils could be hidden even in this short distance; he thought of Johnstone in the whirlpools of the Yuculta Rapids, of Whidbey's party in danger from the landslide, of Barrie and his men poisoned by mussels the previous summer so that one man, John Carter, died; of his own narrow escape from the Indians of Traitor's Cove.

Thinking of these things Vancouver decided, in spite of his illness, to lead the small boat parties himself. He set out, as usual, in the yawl, but within a few hours he was dizzy and very sick, doubled up by stomach cramps, so he had to turn back to *Discovery* and leave Whidbey in charge of the boats. But he ordered the yawl to rejoin Whidbey so that there would be three boats in the party now that they were again near the country where the Indians had proved so treacherous.

Whidbey's first troubles, though it was now the middle of July, were with fog and storms, and with floating ice from the great glaciers around Glacier Bay and along Icy Strait. Once the crews spent the better part of a night fending off the ice to protect the boats, and several times it seemed they would be forced to turn back by ice stretching from shore to shore. But they found a way through somehow and came at last to the clearer waters of Lynn Canal. There they met with Indians again.

At the head of the canal, near the Chilcoot River, the boats were surrounded by a hundred or more Indians who proffered friendship and urged them to go a little way up the river to visit five important chiefs who lived there. Whidbey had no time to make such a visit, even had he not suspected it might be a trap. So he held his boats together and started back down the canal. Very soon they were joined by a war-canoe of twenty Indians, led by a tall, thin old man who was obviously an important chief. He was magnificently dressed in a long cloak of mountain sheep's wool, dyed in several colours and decorated with tufts and fringes; on his head was a wooden helmet, studded with gleaming brass and copper and hung with streamers of dyed wool and ermine. The old man approached Whidbey with great dignity and every sign of friendship, presenting him with a sea-otter skin and gladly accepting some gifts in return. But he would not come aboard the yawl and towards dusk the canoe disappeared.

Whidbey was still suspicious. At nightfall he put into a little cove, but ordered his boats to anchor a short distance from shore and post double guards through the night. In the grey light of early dawn the alarm sounded. Every man was instantly awake and at his post, a loaded musket ready beside him. Five big canoes and several smaller ones, all full of Indians, were paddling straight towards the boats.

Whidbey stood up, his musket held ready, and ordered the canoes to stop. They still came on and the three large canoes closed with the boats. From one the old chief leapt aboard the yawl, a large box in his hand as though he had come to collect plunder. Several of the seamen threw him back into the canoe as the other boats broke up similar attacks. All the canoes then withdrew to some little distance but the men in them were still waving their weapons and shouting threats. Several more canoes came into the bay, until at least two hundred Indians were barring the escape of the boats.

Whidbey ordered the boats to be rowed a little farther from shore, then steadied his men to wait for the attack. It would have been easy to fire a volley and kill a good number of the Indians, but the first attack had been so easily thrown back that Whidbey still hoped to escape without bloodshed, especially as the Indians seemed more inclined to boast and threaten than to attack. The five large canoes, as usual, were steered by old women, but three of them held important chiefs who obviously had full control of the party. One of these, a young, well-built man, brought his canoe close to the yawl. Whidbey counted seven muskets and half a dozen blunderbusses in it, as well as plenty of spears and other weapons. The young chief stood up, a powder horn slung on one shoulder, a spy-glass on the other, shouting threats through a megaphone. As the canoe came close he put down the megaphone, picked up a bright brass blunderbuss and pointed it at Whidbey. Whidbey stood calmly, his own musket ready, and ordered his men to hold their fire. The canoe circled the yawl, then drew away. At this retreat Whidbey ordered his men to row the boats straight out to the middle of the canal. The Indians let them through without resistance, followed a little way, then left. Steady nerves and firm discipline had won out and prevented a fight that could have cost many lives on both sides.

Two days later, not far from the present city of Juneau, the boats were again attacked by Indians. This time two large canoes came up late in the evening, just as they were heading in towards a convenient beach to make camp. The canoes drove ahead to the beach and the Indians jumped out, their spears ready. Once again Widbey had to decide whether or not to fight. There were Indian fires all along the beaches and it was obvious that large settlements were nearby, so he chose to withdraw, keeping the men at the oars all night until they reached country next day where the Indians were friendly. For the first time in the whole survey he had turned back without exploring an inlet to its end.

On Whidbey's safe return to the ships Vancouver moved them on down the broken shores of Chichagof and Baranof Islands and rounded Cape Ommaney to anchor in Port Conclusion, a small sheltered bay near the southern tip of Baranof Island. Again he was too sick to go out with the small boats, but this time it seemed that a week or ten days must join the surveys and finish the work. Ten days passed, then two weeks and they still were not back. Vancouver could only worry and fret in the gloomy weather, under the gloomy mountains of Baranof Island. Had he risked those good men once too often? They had been equal to everything so far, unfailing in nerve and determination and judgment. But fate could turn against even the best of men, and fate had been tempted many times in the three long years along the coast.

The two parties had started out on August 2nd. Johnstone and Barrie went southward to Cape Decision, then on into Sumner Strait to find the mainland again where they had left it the previous year. Whidbey and Swaine turned northward towards Point Gardner at the south end of Admiralty Island, and traced out Stephens Passage to find that it led back to the point where Whidbey had turned away from the warlike Indians on the beach. The Indians were there and waiting again. This time they came in a strong force of large and small canoes, following the boats and closing up with them fast. Whidbey ordered a volley fired over their heads, but they only came on faster, with the largest canoe well in the lead. Whidbey ordered his best marksman to fire a shot directly at the leading canoe. The marksman's aim was good. The canoe stopped immediately, the Indians ducked down under the high gunwales and began paddling as fast as they could towards the other canoes, keeping their high stern directly in line with the boats so that only their hands on the paddles were exposed. Beyond musket range they stopped briefly in consultation, then all the canoes paddled away for the village. Whidbey and his men slept safely ashore that night, though the distant wailing of dirges reached them from the village, suggesting that a chief or some other important man had been killed.

The work held them for several days within reach of the village while they explored Taku Inlet and southward from there through the many arms along the east side of Stephens Passage. By August 16th they had reached Frederick's Sound. It was a lovely morning of warm sunshine after days of heavy rain and the boats put into a sandy beach to dry out clothes and equipment. A party of Indians joined them and seemed friendly at first. Then Whidbey noticed the women and children had disappeared into the bush and the Indians were fastening their daggers on their wrists. He knew it was time to move on.

The Indians followed in canoes for a little way along the opposite shore, then turned off. Supposing he was rid of them, Whidbey decided to land for lunch on a rocky point backed by heavy brush. As soon as the men landed, the canoe appeared again, coming in fast. A shot fired high did not stop it, but a second shot directly at the canoe made the Indians turn off and paddle away round a point.

For some reason Whidbey was still uneasy. He hurried his men through their lunch, got them back in the boats and pushed off as quickly as possible. Almost as soon as they were safely afloat a swarm of Indians, armed with bows and spears, burst out on to the rock behind them. At the same moment the big war-canoe rounded the point again, paddling fast to cut off any retreat. Once again Whidbey and Swaine readied their men; this time a fight seemed certain. Then Swaine waved his arm to the southward and cheered. Johnstone's boats were in sight at no great distance, and coming up fast. The weary men took up Swaine's cheer and the Indians swung away in hurried flight. The great survey was ended. The four boats and the men in them were safe.

Three days later, on August 19th, they reached *Discovery* and *Chatham* in Port Conclusion, to Vancouver's relief and delight. For once he relaxed discipline and allowed his men all the rum they could drink. The celebration went on through the night as the two ships cheered each other, officers and men visited back and forth and the rum flowed in toasts of congratulation and triumph.

In a little while Vancouver withdrew quietly to his cabin under the *Discovery*'s quarter-deck. There he gave

158

thanks to his God for the safety of the men who had served him so well and for the successful ending of the great task he had set himself. He had done far more, he knew, than his orders called for. The great chart, spread out before him, showed a clear and detailed coast-line from lower California to the great Alaskan peninsula. All the confusions and rumours and theories were solved at last. And Cook's reputation stood as proudly as Mount Rainier in Puget Sound or Mt. St. Elias in Alaska. The northwest passage was nowhere south of the arctic icefields.

# 19. Homeward Voyage

THE ships sailed from Port Conclusion in bad weather on August 22nd. Off Cape Ommaney, only a few miles south, the wind failed and a strong tide set them towards a heavy surf breaking along the rocky shore-line. Once more the small boats went overboard and the seamen rowed through the long night to hold the ships from drifting, for there was no bottom for the anchors. Early in the morning a gentle breeze came out of the northwest to save them. But a good seaman was dead. Isaac Wooden, of the cutter's crew, fell overboard and was drowned. As the ships drew away from the coast Vancouver looked back and named tiny Wooden Island as his memorial.

Still hoping to complete his mission there, Vancouver put into Nootka on the way south. He was welcomed by the new governor, Brigadier Alava, who gave him the sad news that his friend Quadra had died in San Blas the previous March. Alava had been sent to Nootka to continue the negotiations, but there were no new orders from either side. The commanders agreed to wait in the port until mid-October; then, as orders still had not come through, they sailed for Monterey.

Vancouver had refitted his ships as best he could at Nootka, but there was still much to be done and his men needed rest and relaxation ashore after eight months of hard sea duty with no fresh food except a few fish from time to time. So he was glad of Alava's friendly invitation to stay at Monterey for as long as he liked and make use of the port in every possible way. But the complete lack of orders from England worried him. It was two years since he had sent back word of his difficulties with Quadra. Had he handled things badly? Had the Lords of the Admiralty lost patience with him? Did they expect him still to fulfil his original orders and arrange a settlement before setting sail for home? He did not know. Yet he had to make a decision. His ships were in no condition to delay through another season.

In the end, instructions came to Alava from the Spanish government. They were secret, but he knew of Vancouver's anxiety and understood the risks that delay would mean for him, so he told him what he knew. The British and Spanish governments had reached an agreement that followed almost exactly the terms Vancouver had held to in his dealing with Quadra; a new British commissioner would be sent out shortly to put it into effect.

As soon as he knew this, Vancouver decided that his duty was done and he was free to sail for England. On December 2nd, 1794, the ships left Monterey on the start of the long voyage home.

The early part of the journey went smoothly and well,

161

with a stop at Cocos Island for fuel and water and fine breezes south of the equator after many days of calm. The *Discovery* crowded on sail and soon left *Chatham* far behind, with a meeting-place set for Juan Fernandez Island off the coast of Chile. Vancouver still hoped there would be time to go on from there and chart the inlets and broken islands southward from Chile to Cape Horn.

For several days the ship raced on under full sail. The sun shone over the white-capped blue water, a steady white wave hissed from her bows and every hour ate away the leagues towards home. Then the wind shifted to the southeast and blew up rain and squalls. A sudden fierce flurry of wind sent the crew aloft to shorten sail. There was a sharp crack, loud above the sounds of the storm, and every man knew the swift, easy days were over. There was a twelve-foot split in the mainmast, starting several feet below the main guy lines. Vancouver took in all sail and at once set to work on repairs. But with the best that could be done the ship could only limp along under shortened sail and, more serious still, she was no longer in shape for the stormy passage round Cape Horn.

Less than a week later Menzies brought word to the quarter-deck that several of the men had scurvy. Vancouver was puzzled and angry. Every man had been in perfect health when they crossed the equator. The water from Cocos Island was good. All Cook's routines of discipline and diet had been faithfully followed. They had been less than four months at sea after all the rest and fresh food at Monterey. Now it seemed that past experience meant little; the disease could still creep in, mysteriously and with all its old deadly effect. Menzies redoubled precautions, but his patients improved little and more men were sick each day.

162

Then the cook, John Brown, came aft to the quarter-deck. He was a serious, steady, reliable man whom Vancouver liked well and trusted completely. But he came now to confess that he had disobeyed orders and served the men boiled beef skimmings with their dried peas ever since leaving Monterey; and he had been doing the same thing two years before, when scurvy broke out between Nootka and Monterey. The men were insistent, he explained, and there was a story among them that the President of the Royal Society in London had said that salt beef skimmings were healthy food and even prevented scurvy.

Vancouver's anger died away in relief. Not only was the outbreak explained, but its cure was easy and certain. He forgave the frightened and penitent John Brown instead of punishing him, then praised him for his honesty. The two "experiments" clearly proved one more disputed point about the disease, and their lesson might well have been lost had John Brown not risked punishment by his confession.

A few days later, in good weather, a sail was sighted astern. It was the *Chatham*, now outsailing the crippled *Discovery*, and Puget came aboard to report to Vancouver as soon as his ship was close enough. He had spoken with a large Spanish merchant vessel a few days before and had learned that Juan Fernandez Island was an open and dangerous anchorage. Valparaiso, on the Chilean coast nearby, was a well-equipped port. Several English ships had put in there recently and had been well received.

Vancouver had strict orders to avoid all Spanish ports in South America except in grave emergency. But he had already decided that he had to replace *Discovery*'s mainmast somehow before risking the passage round Cape Horn, and his sick men needed fresh fruit and vegeta-

163

bles if they were to recover fully. He showed Puget and the other officers the carpenter's reports on the state of the mast and they agreed that the emergency was more than enough to justify putting into Valparaiso.

The two ships anchored in Valparaiso harbour on March 26, 1795. For the first time in four years they were in a port that was a civilized town rather than a garrison settlement, and the town welcomed them. The commandant was Colonel Don Lewis Alava, the brother of Vancouver's friend at Monterey, and he at once sent word of the ships' arrival to President O'Higgins, in the capital city of Santiago.

There was no spar in the port to replace the sprung mainmast, so Vancouver had it taken out of the ship and towed ashore to be strengthened with wooden splints and metal braces, then refitted so that it could be turned end for end and put back in place. The townspeople threw their houses open to both officers and seamen, and kept up a wonderful supply of fresh meat and fruit and vegetables for the sick men aboard the ships. Alava took Vancouver through his warehouses and urged him to pick out all the supplies his ships needed so that they could be released to him as soon as word came back from the capital.

The messengers came back within a few days, bringing permission for Alava to supply everything the ships needed and an urgent invitation from the President for Vancouver and his officers to visit the capital. It was a ninety-mile ride across the hills, but Vancouver decided to go. Alava supplied a dozen or more of the neat little Chilean horses and the President sent two of his Irish Dragoons to guide the expedition along the partly built road between Valparaiso and Santiago.

On the afternoon of the third day they came to the outskirts of the city set on the plain under the high Andes, and Vancouver ordered a stop so that he and his officers could make themselves presentable. They had brought all their best uniforms and linen, but even these were threadbare from use and rotten with the dampness of four long years at sea in tropical heat and sub-arctic cold. The officers ruefully made the best of them, for the honour of England and her navy. Moving gingerly, expecting at any moment to hear the rip and tear of overstrained cloth, they came out of the tents. The President had sent fresh horses, magnificent, spirited creatures, superbly equipped with decorated saddlecloths and saddles and bridles trimmed with gold and silver lace, to carry them in triumph through the city.

The poor seamen took one look at these noble creatures and tried to explain to the Spanish officers who had brought them that their uniforms would never stand the strain of such mounts. The Spanish officers nodded understandingly, disappeared and came back with whips and spurs. The sailors would have no part of these additional hazards, to the distress of their Spanish friends; but they gave in with a good grace and mounted the chargers as bravely as they dared, easing their breeches as gently as possible into the handsome saddles.

All went well and it was a truly triumphal entry, through streets crowded with cheering people all the way to the presidential palace. Here they were received by a guard of honour and shown at once into the great audience chamber, where O'Higgins met them with a simple straightforward welcome that set them immediately at ease.

President Don Ambrosio O'Higgins de Vallenar was an

Irish soldier who had learned his trade in the British army,
then gone to the continent to serve the Spanish King.
Brave and adventurous, an engineer as well as a soldier, he
had quickly made his mark by just and skilful handling of
the southern Indians, and was now pushing forward ambitious plans for development of the country. He was just
the man to appreciate what Vancouver and his people had
achieved, and he questioned them tirelessly on every detail
of the long voyage.

Through the next week the hardworn uniforms were put to the test of an unending succession of levees, dinners, balls and parties of all kinds. All the great houses of the city were thrown open to the visitors and O'Higgins ordered his principal officers to show them everything worth seeing in the city. It was an exciting and inspiring time, made more so by the magnificence of Spanish hospitality and the common interests of men who had discovered new country and those who were settling new country. If O'Higgins asked many questions, he must have answered many too. Vancouver's clear mind and quick eyes, never quicker than when he was studying people and places, carried away an account of the political, military and social life of Chile that filled many pages in his reports and clearly showed his warm admiration for the great President.

Vancouver and his officers returned to Valparaiso on April 16th. On May 6th the ships sailed out of the harbour; three weeks later they rounded Cape Horn in a driving snowstorm and turned northward across the Atlantic towards the Island of St. Helena.

At St. Helena they found themselves in the midst of war between France and Britain. A large convoy of captured merchantmen was just leaving the island under command of the British man-of-war *Sceptre*. As Vancouver landed to pay his respects to the governor he was told that Britain had also declared war against Holland. As he left the governor's mansion a Dutch merchant vessel, the *Macassar*, sailed into the harbour. Without hesitation Vancouver sent one of his officers aboard and made her a prize.

A day or so later the *Chatham*, leaky as she was, battered by the hard trip round the Horn and with half her men disabled by rheumatism, was sent with important dispatches to General Clarke in Brazil. From there she was ordered to come home in the next convoy that sailed for England.

Vancouver sent Johnstone aboard the *Macassar* with orders to bring her home in the next convoy to leave St. Helena. Then he took *Discovery* to sea again, crowding on all sail to come up with the *Sceptre* and her convoy. Just before he left he heard that the French Assembly had granted safe conduct to his ships in recognition of their service, but he knew that word of this might be a long while reaching the French fleets at sea. He set his men to gunnery practice as soon as they were clear of the island and within two or three days *Discovery* was a ship of war and ready to fight her way home if need be. After four years at sea no one aboard had any thought of settling tamely for a spell in the French prison camps.

Captain Essington of the *Sceptre* welcomed Vancouver's ship warmly as she came up with him and put her to work shepherding his scattered, limping convoy. It was hard work and it slowed their passage to the speed of the slowest merchantman. But it was safer than travelling alone and to be on naval duty again was almost like a homecoming in itself, since fair weather and slow sailing made it possible for officers and men to visit from ship to ship.

On September 1st, north of the Azores, bad weather blew up and one of the merchant vessels hoisted a distress signal. *Discovery* went to her at once and found her wallowing deep in the swells. It was soon clear that she had to be abandoned and burned and Vancouver sent the yawl out to do the work, while *Discovery* hove to nearby. Soon the wreck was blazing and the yawl came sliding and twisting over the Atlantic swells with her rescued crew.

Vancouver stood on his quarter-deck, watching as the men scrambled safely up the heaving side of the ship. Blocks were dropped from the boom and hooked to the ring-bolts and the yawl was hoisted clear of the water. Just at that moment a great wave broke and smashed the little boat in pieces against the *Discovery*'s side.

For a moment Vancouver stood quite still, remembering a hundred expeditions, a hundred dangers, a hundred safe returns, from Dusky Bay to Traitor's Cove to the grinding ice-floes of Cook's Inlet. Then he turned away to hide the tears he could not hold back. It seemed that a great part of his life had been suddenly scattered there on the tossing Atlantic with the bones of the little yawl.

# 20. The Last Duty

THE *Discovery* moored in the Shannon River, on the west coast of Ireland, in mid-September, and Vancouver went directly from there to report to the Admiralty. From London, he went briefly to King's Lynn to visit his brother John and his sisters, but by the middle of October *Discovery* had sailed round to Deptford, on the Thames and he was aboard her again.

There was much to be done. Years earlier a return from such a voyage might have brought a hero's welcome. Now it was one more small routine in the expansion of empire, almost lost in the excitement of the war with France. Vancouver found that his men were taken up by the navy press-gangs as soon as they were paid off and sent ashore. He took their case to the Admiralty. After four and a half years of hard sea duty they were entitled to time ashore with their friends and families, war or no war. They were all good men who had served him well and would serve the navy again in due time. He wanted them released to shore leave. The Admiralty sent word to the Admiral in the Downs and the men were released.

Before the end of October orders came through for the reposting of all the master's mates and midshipmen of the *Discovery* to the warship *Caroline.* Again Vancouver wrote Evan Nepean of the Admiralty. These men had put in their time and were entitled to write the examinations for promotion to commissioned rank. Again, they were good men and not one had the least intention of leaving the service. Nepean at his desk read over the list of names. "Orders accordingly," he wrote briefly. "Let him know it." Ten of the *Discovery*'s young gentlemen immediately wrote examinations for promotion, and more than one of them later went on to flag rank in the Royal Navy.

These were important and urgent affairs. There were many others, which took Vancouver's full time over the next several months. Then, early in 1796, he was ordered by the Admiralty to write the full acount of his voyage for publication. In this again he was following Cook's tradition, and he turned to the work gladly, though his health was failing very fast.

Though he was a practical seaman, more used to action than words, no one understood better than Vancouver the importance of the work he had to do. The world, he believed, was owed a full and honest account of everything he had seen and done. He was determined it should have it so exactly and precisely, with such unfailing honesty, that there would be no room whatsoever for the arm-chair critics who had dogged Cook and attempted to lessen his memory. The northwest coast-line was explored down to its last significant detail; the claims and counterclaims, the rumours and fantasies of a northwest passage within the latitudes of practical navigation had been for ever disposed of; and the world must know it.

Hoping to strengthen himself for the work, he spent a short while at the hot sulphur baths in Bristol, then settled in a small cottage at the village of Petersham in Surrey. His brother John came down from London to keep him company and help with the work; and the next two years, in spite of his sickness, were among the happiest of his life. Petersham was a quiet and lovely place, with views over a settled countryside of villages and church spires and mansions and farm lands, just such a countryside as he had again and again imagined in the beautiful setting of Puget Sound and the other wild places he had discovered. His sickness gave him great surges of energy and optimism, even while it drained his strength and wore him down. When he was too sick to write, John wrote the words down as he dictated them.

By May of 1798, all but the last few pages were written. George Vancouver was very sick, but he was at peace. He had lived his life for his country and for the navy that had raised him from boyhood. He had carried on and vindicated the work of his great commander. He had written of his voyage honestly and completely, so that the work would stand for all time. It remained only to find the ending and this was already written in his rough notes of the voyage, which his brother John was sorting under the open window on that warm May evening. It was a last remembrance of the men, great and small, who had made the real story of the voyage.

There were many to remember: Johnstone and Whidbey, who had borne the brunt of the work; the faithful Broughton even now returned to more exploration in the

Pacific; Zach. Mudge who thought promotion far too slow; Peter Puget; the reliable Manby; and promising young fellows like Robert Barrie, Spelman Swaine and Edward Roberts. Old Menzies, too, with his plants and his glass house on the *Discovery*'s quarter-deck had been faithful and wise, though difficult at times.

He remembered Pomurrey and Tamaahmaah, beloved friends whom he would never see again. And Quadra above all, brave seaman, courtly Spanish gentleman, generous host, the warmest of friends even in disagreement.

Then, too, there were the men who had died because of the expedition. Several—too many—of the innocent native peoples. One man in the Chatham Islands; two whole years without a shot fired in anger, then the unknown number of deaths at Traitor's Cove and perhaps two others, not more than two, on Whidbey's last trip in the small boat. Unnecessary deaths, all of them, the unhappy yield of misunderstanding or faulty judgment, yet unavoidable in the precise conditions that brought them about.

Lastly there were those of his own men whose bones lay scattered on the sea floor or buried in the wild places. He remembered them all, one by one in the quiet of the English countryside they had not lived to see again. John Brown, carpenter's mate, drowned as they sailed from the Channel in 1791; Neil Coil, the marine, dead of dysentery beyond the Cape of Good Hope in the same year; Joseph Murgatroyd, carpenter, missing at sea in January of 1793; John Carter, seaman, killed by poisoned mussels in the same year; Isaac Wooden, lost off Wooden Island as they turned for home; Richard Jones, seaman, swept overboard in a storm just north of Cape Horn on the homeward voyage. Six men from a crew of a hundred in four hard years of danger; from the *Chatham*, not one man had been lost. And of the others, every man had reached home in perfect health and full strength. There was much to be thankful for and George Vancouver folded his hands and solemnly thanked his God.

When the light failed on that warm May evening and John turned from his papers at the window, there was one more name to add to *Discovery*'s casualty list: George Vancouver, Captain and Commander. At forty, after twenty-five long years at sea, his work was done.